Taste of Life
COOKBOOK

Taste of Life
COOKBOOK

200 Low Cholesterol Easy to Make Healthy Life Style Recipes

Julie Stafford

AUSTRALIA In Print

Taste of Life Cookbook
First published in 1989 by
Australia In Print Inc.
110 W. Ocean Blvd., Suite 537
Long Beach, CA 90802

ISBN 0 7328 0009 9

The recipes collected here
were selected from Julie Stafford's
three cookbooks published in Australia by
Greenhouse Publications Pty Ltd
54 Park Street, Sydney, NSW 2000

Taste of Life
First printing 1983
Reprinted 1984 (six times)
Reprinted 1985 (twice)
Reprinted 1986 (three times)
Reprinted 1987
Reprinted 1988

More Taste of Life
First printing 1985
Reprinted 1985
Reprinted 1987

Taste of Life for Children
First printing 1986

Typeset in Australia by Dead Set
Printed and bound in Australia by Griffin Press
Book and cover design Sandra Nobes
Cover photography Phil Wymant and Ann Creber
Photographs Phil Wymant except for page 117
taken by Paul Tremelling
Drawings Lowana Cummin

Unless the doctors of today become the dietitians of tomorrow, the dietitians of today will become the doctors of tomorrow.

– Alexis Carrel
Nobel Prize Winner (1935)

Blessed is the man who enjoys the small things, the common beauties, the little day by day events;
Sunshine on the fields, birds on the bough,
Breakfast, dinner, supper, the daily paper on the porch, a friend passing by.
So many people who go afield for enjoyment, leave it behind them at home.

– David Grayson,
The Friendship Book

Very little is needed to make a happy healthy life.
It is all within yourself, in your way of thinking and eating.

… If you have your health, you have everything …

Keep your diet within your body's means and remember the following:

    The value of Time
    The success of Perseverance
    The pleasure of Working
    The dignity of Simplicity
    The worth of Character
    The power of Example
    The influence of Life
    The obligation of Duty
    The wisdom of Economy
    The virtue of Patience
    The improvement of Talent
    The joy of Originating

I found these words on the wall of a restaurant in San Francisco, and I thought how wonderful life could be if we all took time to make these simple factors the major factors of our daily lives. Happiness and health surely would result in the harmony of life.

For Bruce, Timothy and Cassie,
for you are my most precious possessions —
and your health is your most precious possession.

INFORMATION ABOUT THE FOODS IN THIS BOOK

The foods in this book are low in fats, low in cholesterol and low in protein – especially animal protein. They offer plenty of nutrition and much needed fiber. There is no added refined sugar or salt, and no added preservatives or artificial flavors in any of the recipes. The foods include:

- vegetables
- fruits
- legumes
- grains
- a small amount of nuts (almonds and pinenuts)
- a small amount of seeds (sesame and sunflower seeds for added flavor)
- natural sun dried fruits
- non-fat and some low fat dairy products
- a small amount of lean, fat free red meat, chicken and fish

CONTENTS

I NTRODUCTION

I would like to share a little of myself with you, for I am not on the list of the world's greatest chefs, nor am I a student of the famous Cordon Bleu cooking schools. I will, however, promise you mouth-watering delights to start you on the road to your improved state of health. My cooking ability, and collection of recipes are newly acquired after much research into diet related to health. It was not until my husband, at the age of thirty years, was diagnosed as having cancer that I began my research into diet related to disease, but most of all, in diet related to an overall state of health.

The dangers of high cholesterol are well documented. There is now overwhelming evidence that the higher the blood cholesterol level the greater is the risk of developing cardio-vascular disease.

I believe that today's statistics show that almost half the population of America is in the risk category for cardio-vascular disease.

Taste of Life Cookbook is a collection of my favorite recipes all of which are low in fat and cholesterol, and salt and sugar free. I stress the use of wholegrain cereals and the freshest possible natural ingredients with no artificial flavoring or coloring.

I began to develop this collection of recipes when, at the age of thirty, my husband was diagnosed with Hodgkins Disease, a cancer of the lymphatic system. At that time we were living on a farm and our diet was high in fats, cholesterol, sugar and salt, and low in complex carbohydrate foods.

I felt that our diet may have been a contributing factor to his disease and that by making some changes he might have a fighting chance of survival. The conventional treatments of chemotherapy and radiation had had a devastating effect on his once healthy body and my aim was to introduce a new diet which would help his body eliminate these chemical poisons.

The diet was at first made up almost entirely of unadulterated fruits and vegetables. As he slowly recovered, wholegrain cereals and small quantities of lean meat were added and we began to realize we had created a new dietary lifestyle for ourselves.

We called it 'Taste of Life' because for us it was a completely new taste sensation and it was also a new life for Bruce. In 1985, within three years of the original diagnosis, he was given the 'all clear' and today maintains an excellent state of health.

The whole family eat 'Taste of Life' food and we all feel better for it. I find it easy to maintain my correct weight and we all have greatly increased energy levels.

One of the advantages of changing over to this type of dietary lifestyle is that the benefits are felt so quickly. It is also an easy regime to follow and the food tastes so good that the whole family will be readily converted.

The foods I encourage you to eat and the methods of cooking I recommend in this book are similar to those recommended by health organizations throughout the world. They are foods which I believe will reduce your chances of developing many of the diseases which plague our society today including many types of cancer, the adult onset of diabetes, obesity, constipation, hypertension, kidney disease, gallstones, diverticular disease, arthritis and other debilitating disorders.

I sincerely hope that this book will help you in your search for improved good health and that, as well, you will enjoy a whole range of new taste sensations.

Good eating and good health,
Julie Stafford.

CHOLESTEROL
IT'S A KILLER!

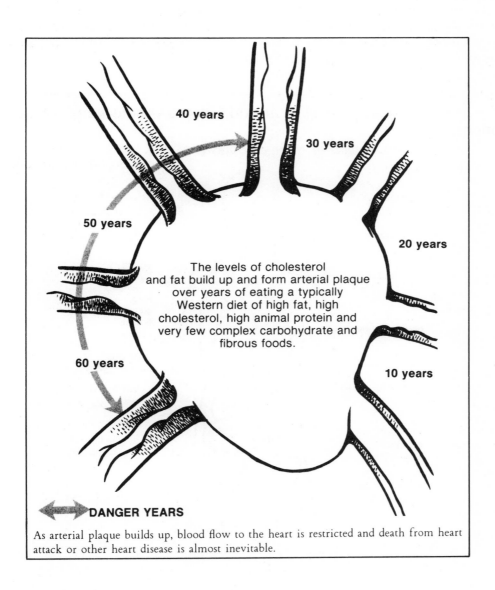

40 years

30 years

50 years

20 years

The levels of cholesterol and fat build up and form arterial plaque over years of eating a typically Western diet of high fat, high cholesterol, high animal protein and very few complex carbohydrate and fibrous foods.

60 years

10 years

DANGER YEARS

As arterial plaque builds up, blood flow to the heart is restricted and death from heart attack or other heart disease is almost inevitable.

HOW TO AVOID DEGENERATIVE DISEASES

Eat well. The human body must be the greatest machine of all. It is a delicate system of connected pipes and organs which, when fed the proper quality and quantity of fuel, perform the most extraordinary tasks. High quality food allows the human body to work most effectively.

Exercise well. Exercising develops healthy muscles and tissues and ensures better blood circulation and an adequate flow of oxygen to vital organs. This provides increased energy and stamina, increased flexibility, coordination and body control. Exercises also make you feel great!

Rest well. The body needs sleep and quiet times to regenerate energy.

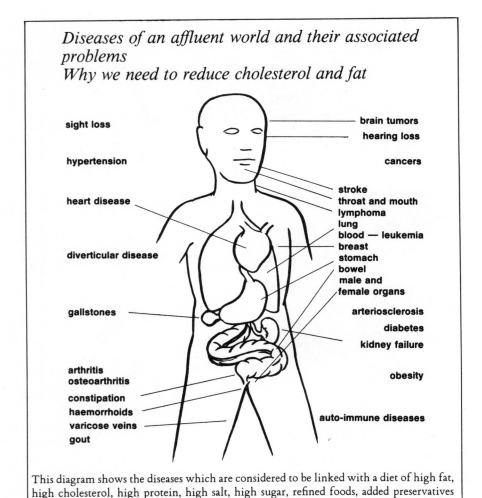

Diseases of an affluent world and their associated problems
Why we need to reduce cholesterol and fat

sight loss

brain tumors

hearing loss

hypertension

cancers

stroke
throat and mouth
lymphoma
lung
blood — leukemia
breast
stomach
bowel
male and
female organs

heart disease

diverticular disease

gallstones

arteriosclerosis

diabetes

kidney failure

arthritis
osteoarthritis

obesity

constipation
haemorrhoids
varicose veins
gout

auto-immune diseases

This diagram shows the diseases which are considered to be linked with a diet of high fat, high cholesterol, high protein, high salt, high sugar, refined foods, added preservatives and food colorings.

NUTRITION

Nutrition sustains the body. The food we eat utilizes the energy it provides; it is the fuel that operates the machine. Good nutrition depends on how wisely we choose the food we eat. A combination of complex carbohydrates, proteins, fats, vitamins and minerals is essential and should be provided by our diet.

Complex carbohydrates: These are the body's source of energy. Sugar is perhaps the most commonly known carbohydrate but it is a refined carbohydrate with more harmful than beneficial effects. Refined, it is stripped of the fiber and nutrition value. Sugar includes sucrose (table sugar), lactose (milk sugar), fructose (fruit sugar), honey and glucose. The average American consumes sugar in excess – more than two pounds of sugar per week. Excess sugar in the diet can be directly linked with obesity, diabetes, hypertension, hypoglycemia and artero-sclerosis (an early sign of heart disease). It provides a lot of calories with few nutrients.

Unrefined carbohydrates or complex carbohydrates which include the starch-rich natural foods like grains, roots, vegetables and fruits, are an excellent source of energy.

The body takes longer to break down complex carbohydrates. Therefore it can tolerate the level of glucose being absorbed into the bloodstream at the one time. Another bonus with complex carbohydrates is that they contain essential fiber which is beneficial for good health. When fiber is lacking from the diet, health problems like constipation, haemorrhoids, appendicitis, hiatus hernia and colon cancer are evident.

In the early twentieth century modern technology provided machines to refine a lot of foods. It enabled us to create the six inch high sponge filled with cream, the three inch high scones to serve with jam and cream, the French croissant to fill with ham and cheese, the snowiest of white bread and so on. The shelves of bakehouses never looked so good, but we forgot that food nutrients are an essential part of survival. In many cases we have milled the goodness out of the food, leaving a visual delight but a nutrition-lacking disaster.

Proteins: The body requires protein to build new cells and repair damaged tissues, and to help maintain body tissues. Grains, roots, vegetables and fruits in an unrefined, minimally processed form are an excellent source of protein. These foods are a much better source of protein than animal foods such as meat, fish, eggs and milk which usually have very high fat content.

Fiber: Fiber's function is to create bulk in the intestine and move faeces through the system quickly to avoid the build-up of toxins in the body. Excess fiber in the diet can interfere with the absorption of some minerals and vitamins. Some recipes in this book have taken into account the amount of fiber in a given recipe and have been regulated accordingly (cakes, cookies, breads, muffins). Unbleached, chemical free, preservative free flour has been added to some of these recipes to reduce the possibility of excessive fiber for children.

Water: Water is just as essential as other nutrients, if not more essential. The body requires anywhere between four and eight glasses of water per day so that it can effectively carry out its bodily functions. Water helps to provide a means of transport for nutrients to be carried through the body, and for wastes and toxins to be expelled from the body. Water also helps to maintain body temperature.

STOCKING THE LARDER

Almonds: These are the only nuts used in the recipes. Although almonds have a high fat content, they are a high quality, nutritious food. However, to reduce fat intake in the diet it is important to keep recipes containing almonds to a minimum. Use those recipes for special occasions. Almonds are best bought in their shells and shelled as required. Unshelled nuts are protected from heat, air, light and moisture and' will keep almost indefinitely.

Shredded coconut: Coconuts are an excellent source of phosphorus and potassium but are high in fat. A small amount is occasionally called for to flavor a recipe but use sparingly.

Pinenuts, sunflower seeds, poppy seeds, pumpkin kernels and sesame seeds: These are used very sparingly to flavor some recipes. All can be bought at health food shops.

Vanilla essence: The pure vanilla essence is obtained by steeping the vanilla pods in alcohol (usually brandy) and water over a period of time.

Canned and packaged foods: Use canned and packaged foods only when fresh food is not available or is too expensive. Become a label reader! Look for natural food, without sugar, salt or other additives. It is one thing to save a few cents on an item with all the additives, but it is later in life that the cost becomes a burden.

Ginger: Peel the root before chopping up very finely. To make fresh ginger juice, place small pieces in a garlic crusher and squeeze. It is used to flavor many dishes, spicy and sweet. It is also reputed to be an excellent remedy for sore throats and stomach upsets.

Garlic: This bulbous plant of the onion family is composed of many small cloves enclosed in a papery skin. It has a long history of uses, both culinary and medicinal and is said to be one of nature's most natural antibiotics. It has a very pungent flavor and enhances many dishes.

Soy sauce: A dark, almost black, thin sauce made from fermented soya beans. It enhances vegetable, meat and rice dishes. Use only a low salt variety.

Herbs: These are best grown fresh in your garden but you should also explore and decide which varieties suit your palate. These can be used individually or combined to create wonderful flavors in sweet or spicy recipes without the need to add salt or sugar.

Tofu: This is soya bean curd. It is made by adding a natural coagulant (lemon juice) to soy milk. Curds are created, the excess milk drained off and it is pressed into block form to remove all liquid. It has an excellent protein and calcium content, is low in fat and is cholesterol free. Tofu has a bland taste and can be used for salads, sweet or savory dishes.

Brown rice: Brown rice is the natural, unpolished rice that has been hulled but still has its bran. The bran in brown rice offers additional protein, plus traces of iron, calcium and vitamin B. It has a nutty flavor and is extremely nutritious. It takes longer to cook than white rice.

Dried fruits: These include apricots, apples,

raisins, currants, bananas, peaches, nectarines and pears. Dried fruits contain a high level of natural sugar, so they should not be eaten in excess. Look for sun dried fruits without additives where possible.

Tomato paste: This is a concentrated purée of tomatoes. You can make your own tomato paste by peeling and deseeding very ripe tomatoes. Chop them up finely and cook until they thicken. Do not add any liquid.

Chicken stock: Boil up some chicken carcasses and/or meat in a combination of water and orange juice. Add onion, celery, carrot and ginger root or garlic. Let simmer for two hours. Strain, cool and deglaze. Use as required.

Vegetable stock: Combine mixed vegetables and spices, cover with water and simmer for 2 hours. Strain and cool.

Sprouts: Alfalfa sprouts are the most common, but mung beans and lentils are also excellent sprouted. Buy ready sprouted or sprout your own. Alfalfa sprouts are rich in nearly all vitamins and minerals. They are a good source of protein and enzymes, as are most other sprouts.

Agar: This is a seaweed based setting agent like gelatin. It is high in protein and calcium and easy to digest. For all recipes in this book granulated agar is used. One teaspoon of agar sets approximately one cup of liquid, depending on the texture you require.

Yeast: Baker's yeast in granulated form is used in all recipes to act as a leavener for breads and pizza dough.

Natex: This is a low salt yeast extract. It contains no artificial additives or preservatives. Use on toast or in sandwiches.

Vecon: This is a concentrated vegetable stock with vitamins. It makes a quick vegetable stock when reconstituted with water. The amount will be determined by the flavor required. Add it to casseroles, soups and gravies when a suitable stock is not available.

Peppermint extract: This is a concentrated oil from the steaming distillation of the peppermint plant.

Orange and lemon extract: These are concentrated extracts of the fruits. Use pure essences and use them sparingly.

Skim milk powder: This is milk from which the moisture has been removed. It is added to dry ingredients or reconstituted by adding water.

Non-fat or skim milk: This is milk with less than 1 per cent milk fat. It still contains the nutrients of whole milk except for fat soluble vitamins.

Evaporated low fat milk: This is canned milk with a large percentage of water removed. It contains no sugar, has a heavier texture than non-fat milk, and is a good substitute in recipes calling for whole milk. It is pure skim milk with 60 per cent of water removed and contains less than $1/2$ per cent fat.

Non-fat buttermilk: Originally, buttermilk was the liquid drained from the churn after butter making. Today buttermilk is made by adding selected bacteria to non-fat milk. It is slightly acidic in flavor, thicker in consistency than milk, and thinner than yogurt. Nutritionally it compares with skim milk with a maximum fat content of around 0.8 per cent. Buttermilk can be substituted for milk in any recipe.

Low fat ricotta cheese: This is made from the curd rather than the liquid milk, which is drained off. It has a bland flavor and is a mass of fine, small curd particles. It is suitable to add to savory or sweet dishes and is delicious just as it is on vegetable crudités, wholemeal bread or wholemeal crackers. Preferably look for cheese with 1 per cent fat content

Non-fat cottage cheese: This cheese has the consistency of paste and has a light acidic flavor though it is still fairly bland. It contains a maximum of about 0.4 per cent fat. Again, it is suitable for savory or sweet dishes.

Wholemeal flour: All recipes in this book which include wholemeal flour (or cake flour) refer to 80 per cent wholemeal flour (or cake flour). One hundred per cent wholemeal may be used. One hundred per cent wholemeal flour contains the highest nutrient and protein value, as well as bran for essential fiber.

Unbleached white flour: This is wholemeal flour with the bran and husks removed, but without the addition of chemicals. Use in conjunction with wholemeal flour for baking or substitute half or all with 80 per cent wholemeal flour.

Eggs: Egg whites are used in a number of recipes. Egg yolks contain fat and cholesterol and are rarely used. The egg white, when whipped to form stiff peaks, breaks down protein and these expand, forming elastic walled cells that trap air. This in turn expands when subjected to heat. This is what makes egg whites such a valuable leavening agent. Yolk protein, on the other hand, binds and thickens. It can be substituted by doubling the egg whites for the number of eggs in a recipe or by adding a small amount of another thickening and binding ingredient like arrowroot, grated or cooked apple or fresh banana.

Wholemeal bread: Choose those varieties that are salt free or low in salt, sugar free and oil free or low in oil. Those breads containing grains are an excellent choice. Introduce variations in bread types such as rye bread and sourdough. Making your own bread is one sure way of knowing what actually goes into the bread. There are wholemeal, salt free bread mixes now available in supermarkets and health food stores.

Wholemeal pita bread: Also known as flatbread or Lebanese bread, it is basically made from wholemeal flour, water and minimal salt. It is excellent just as it is or filled with salad ingredients. It also makes an excellent pizza base.

Wholemeal filo pastry: This is excellent for wrapping food. Dry bake in the oven until filling is cooked and pastry is crisp. Because it is paper thin you will need several sheets of pastry to make a layer for the base of a pie.

Fruit juices: The best quality juices are obtained by juicing fresh fruits and vegetables and returning fruit fiber to the liquid. When buying fruit juices choose those that do not have sugar added to them and are preservative free. Do not overuse juices. Encourage children to drink plenty of water from an early age.

Herb teas: There is much nutritional value in herb teas. Children will enjoy them chilled with ice cubes and slices of lemon or lime.

Caro: This is a cereal beverage made of roasted, malted barley, chicory and rye. For children who like a hot drink with Mom and Dad, it is an excellent choice. It is caffeine free.

Carob: This is a fine dark powder. It comes from carob pods (from carob trees) which are deseeded, toasted and ground to make a sweet tasting flavoring agent. Add to cakes and treats, drinks and desserts. Use slightly more carob in recipes when substituting it for cocoa. Carob contains natural sugar. It is caffeine free, so it is preferable to chocolate or cocoa.

Apple juice concentrate: This is apple juice boiled down to a syrup. It can be reconstituted to an apple juice drink by adding water. 'Apple juice is preferred to honey because it contains vitamins, minerals and water soluble fiber (pectin) which honey does not have. Honey is approximately 80 per cent sugar and apple juice concentrate is approximately 66 per cent. Honey has 61 calories per tablespoon and apple juice concentrate has 30 calories per tablespoon.' (Nutrition Department, Pritikin Longevity Center.)

Cold oil: When oil is extracted with little or no heat or use of chemical solvents, as for ordinary oils, the vitamin E content is not destroyed. Oil should be bought in brown bottles or cans, kept away from light and refrigerated. Do not use oil excessively and only in the amounts given in the recipes. I use almond oil for sweet cooking or grapeseed oil, and use recipes containing oil in moderation.

Sodium-free baking powder: All recipes in this book using flour and baking powder use commercially packaged baking powder. To maintain a diet low in sodium you can make your own sodium-free baking powder by using equal quantities of the following ingredients:

2 tablespoons cornstarch
2 tablespoons cream of tartar
2 tablespoons potassium bicarbonate
(available at drug stores).

Sift ingredients together and store in an airtight jar. Shake before using. Use approximately two teaspoons of this baking powder for every one cup of flour. The baking powder will begin to react once it combines with moisture so you need to work quickly at this stage, placing it in the oven before it subsides.

Note: A better result in your baking of cakes may be achieved by increasing oven temperature and reducing cooking time (5 minutes).

Oat Bran: Oat bran is obtained by taking the whole grain, steaming it, passing it between rollers (rolled oats), then grinding it. This results in a fine oat flour and a coarser particle which is the oat bran. Oat bran contains water soluble fiber and it is this fiber which is associated with a lowering of cholesterol levels.

HERBS AND SPICES

'Using a little is better than a lot' – herbs are meant to complement a dish, not dominate it.

Allow quarter of a teaspoon of dried herbs for each four servings.

Crush herb in the palm of your hand before adding. This gives quicker flavor release.

Uncooked foods such as salad dressings, fruits and juices need time for the flavors to integrate properly, so add them as long before serving as possible.

Do not combine too many herbs at one time. Few herbs complement each other.

If in doubt, use only one.

One herb course to a meal is plenty.

The right herb to use is always the herb that's right for you. Only after experimentation will you become familiar with their strengths and delicacies.

When using dried herbs instead of fresh, the flavor is more concentrated, so use a lot less.

Herbs are very easy to grow, inside or out.

Never oven dry herbs. Hang them in bundles in a cool place or place on brown paper in a dark cupboard to dry.

HERBS

Basil: sweet basil has light green, soft leaves. Wild basil has much smaller leaves. When broken and rubbed in the fingers, the foliage has a spicy aroma like cloves. Sweet basil has a slightly stronger perfume than wild basil.

Use: fresh or dry leaves go into Italian dishes, season tomatoes, eggplant, pepper, vegetable soups, tomato sauce. The fresh leaves are excellent in a tossed salad, potato salad, rice salad, cucumber, or cooked green bean salad. Basil is one of the most useful herbs.

Bay leaves: a bay leaf is added to a bouquet garni, the other herbs being thyme, marjoram and parsley. It is used to flavor marinades, stocks, soups, poultry and fish dishes. Bay leaves may be used fresh or dried, but should be kept in an airtight container.

Balm or lemon balm: this herb has a very strong lemon scent. The leaves are oval in shape and crinkly like spearmint.

Use: fresh leaves are floated on top of cool drinks. Delicious chopped into fruit salad. They give a lemon tang to a tossed green salad. Fresh or dried lemon balm may be put into a teapot with tea as a refreshing pick-me-up.

Borage: this herb has broad, hairy leaves with a cucumber flavor.

Use: when chopped very finely, they make fillings for sandwiches and are good to add to tossed salads. The whole young leaves go into cool drinks.

Caraway: frond-like leaves. The pungent seeds are rich in aromatic oils, and are prized for their use in cooking and as an aid to digestion. Store seed in an airtight container.

Use: breads, especially rye bread. They flavor soups, stewed and baked fruits such as apples and pears. They flavor vegetables such as cabbage, carrots and cauliflower.

Chervil: the green foliage resembles a fine leafed parsley and has a delicate aniseed taste.

Use: the chopped fresh or dried leaves go into the classic 'fines herbes', which comprises equal proportions of chervil, tarragon, parsley and chives. Put in mashed potatoes, green salads, white sauce for fish or poultry.

Chives: onion chives have a round, hollow leaf with a mild flavor of onion. Garlic chives have a flat leaf broader than onion chives and are not such a dark green. The flavor is mildly garlic.

Use: the chopped chives go into salads, cottage cheese and can be used as a garnish for baked potatoes, soups, entrées, fish and sauces.

Coriander: has lacy, feathery foliage. Ripe coriander seeds are slightly oval, small and a beige color. It has a spicy aroma.

Use: the ground seeds are used to give a tang to fish, poultry and meat dishes. They flavor cakes, cookies, pastries and bread. Sprinkle a little ground coriander over apples, pears and peaches while baking. A pinch flavors eggplant and peppers.

Dill: has delicate leaves of dark green aromatic foliage. Seeds have a pungently dry aromatic flavor (aniseed).

Use: the foliage, either the fresh chopped leaves or the dried crumbled leaves, flavors dips, spreads, sauces, salad dressings, coleslaw, tossed green salads, potato salad, fish and rice. Sprinkle lightly on vegetables. The seeds flavor pickles, chutney, coleslaw, steamed fish, meat loaf, potato salad, cottage cheese, cabbage, cauliflower and cucumber. Dill is an excellent herb used with seafood.

Fennel: the foliage when fresh is chopped finely and sprinkled over fish while cooking, or the whole leaves are used as a stuffing for fish.

Use: the seeds, which have digestive properties, go into pastries and breads, into

fish and meat dishes and can be added to steamed cabbage while cooking. They are excellent in beet or potato salads.

Garlic: this pungent herb is used in a tremendous number of dishes, particularly casseroles, salads and sauces.

Lovage: the tasty, beneficial leaves of this plant give flavor to soups, vegetables and salads.

Marjoram: oregano and marjoram are closely related herbs.

Use: in pasta and rice dishes, pizza, tomatoes, eggplant, pepper, zucchini, some meat dishes and savory sauces.

Mint: a refreshing herb with a cool, clean flavor.

Use: in cool drinks. Excellent with citrus fruit and pineapple, orange and onion salad, new potatoes, peas, carrots, tomato sauces, mint sauce, tomatoes.

Oregano: has a far more pungent flavor than marjoram. It is used with pasta, rice, tomatoes, eggplant, peppers, zucchini, in pizzas and savory sauces, and also in some meat dishes.

Parsley: a long time favorite for many reasons. It has attractive leaves useful for garnishes. It has a pleasing taste and contains many health-giving vitamins and minerals. It is also an excellent breath deodorizer after garlic and onions. It combines excellently with chopped chives.

Use: as a garnish or chopped in soups, over salads, vegetables, pasta dishes, rice and mashed potatoes.

Rosemary: the oil in the leaves is very pungent, so use sparingly at first.

Use: chop leaves fresh or dried and add them to stuffings for meat or chicken. Add to potato pastry, spinach, carrots, zucchini, eggplant.

Sage: this is one of the ingredients in mixed herbs, the others being marjoram and thyme.

Use: in stuffing with onions. It seasons breadcrumbs for chicken or fish.

Salad burnet: this herb has soft, serrated fern-like leaves which have a mild flavor of cucumber.

12

Use: leaves go into tossed salads and iced drinks, and are delicious finely chopped for herb sandwiches.

Winter savory: the foliage has a peppery flavor. Savory dries easily and will keep its true flavor for a time if stored in air tight containers.

Use: the peppery taste flavors rissoles, savory mince, beans and pea soups, sauces and salads. The chopped leaves can be sprinkled over cooked marrows, zucchini, squash, beans.

Tarragon: a strong flavored herb, a little goes a long way. The French tarragon is recommended for culinary use. It does not set seeds. Tarragon must be dried quickly to keep its color and flavor.

Use: the spicy, somewhat tart taste of the leaves gives a piquant flavor to poultry and fish. Add to a wine vinegar and keep aside for a dressing.

Thyme: garden thyme is the kind most used in cooking. Thyme can be picked throughout the year to use fresh in cooking. Thyme is an ingredient in mixed herbs, together with sage and marjoram.

Use: it seasons meat loaf, rissoles, stews, soups and strongly flavored vegetables like onions, steamed cabbage, rutabaga, turnips and parsnips. Thyme makes an excellent herb tea.

THE SPICE THAT'S RIGHT

Allspice: a spice which has an aroma similar to a combination of cinnamon, cloves and nutmeg. The flavor is strong, so it should be used sparingly.

Use: to flavor chutneys, relish, marinades, cakes and steamed puddings.

Cayenne: a ground spice of the chilli pepper family.

Use: sparingly to flavor seafood, sauces, or as an interesting addition to a basic coleslaw.

Chillies: these can be whole dried or finely ground.

Use: to add flavor to curries or chutneys or rice dishes.

Cinnamon: this spice is the bark of a tree native to Ceylon. It is presented in a rolled up quill form or finely ground. It is possibly one of the most popular spices.

Use: adds flavor to rice dishes, curries, cooked fruits such as apples, apricots or pears, cakes and steamed puddings. Cinnamon and orange juice added to a natural yogurt make a delicious, refreshing summer dessert.

Cloves: a spice with a powerful flavor used very sparingly.

Use: whole cloves or ground cloves are excellent when cooking apples and pears, chutneys, steamed puddings, dried fruits and some vegetable dishes.

Coriander: a spice which comes in seed or ground form. It has an orange-like flavor and adds zest to a rice dish or to curries.

Ginger: a spicy warm flavor. For meat and vegetable dishes it is usually teamed with other spices. For desserts, cakes and steamed puddings it should be used sparingly.

Mace: is the outer casing of nutmeg. It has a similar flavor to nutmeg but is slightly more refined. Half a teaspoon of mace is equal to a quarter of a teaspoon of nutmeg.

Use: to flavor soups, vegetable casseroles, sauces, stuffings.

Mustard: comes in seed or powder form. Its flavor is pleasantly piquant.

Use: to add flavor to a white sauce, a mayonnaise or vegetable dishes.

Nutmeg: is most suitably used fresh and grated to capture its true flavor.

Use: a widely used spice in hot or cold drinks, spicy or sweet dishes. Try it with fish, veal, spinach, carrots, cakes and cooked fruits.

Paprika: spice used for its flavor and color. It is the ground seed of the sweet pepper and ranges from mild to sweet to mildly hot.

Use: flavors chicken, vegetables, fish and sauces. Its bright red color sprinkled over a pale dish immediately adds warmth and interest.

Peppercorns: I prefer to use whole black peppercorn, freshly ground.

Use: to add flavor to all meat and vegetable dishes. Black peppercorns are dry, hard and very hot. Green and red peppercorns are soft to touch and not as strong in flavor.

COOKING TIPS

A steamer of some sort is a desirable aid in the cooking of vegetables. If you do not have one, improvise with pans — sit a small rack on the bottom of the pan about 2–3 inches from the base. Make sure lids fit tightly so you do not lose valuable nutrients in escaping steam. A simple method of steaming is to wrap food securely in foil. This parcel can then be cooked in the oven or barbecued.

A stiff nailbrush is a useful tool for scrubbing vegetables when it is not necessary to completely remove the skins.

For easy peeling of garlic, place garlic on a hard board and press down with a knife to bruise the garlic. Skin will peel off easily in your fingers.

When stir frying in a small amount of water or stock, add the strongest flavors first (e.g. onions, garlic). This will break down the fibers and develop a sauce.

Cut down the acidity in tomato recipes by removing all the seeds.

Remove the pith from oranges and use only the colored flesh. The pith is extremely bitter, especially if you are cooking oranges.

Gluten is the protein from wheat. Five teaspoons of gluten should be used to four cups of flour to make an elastic bread dough.

Wholemeal or rye flours absorb more moisture than white flour, so if adapting old recipes keep this in mind.

Vinegar in chutney will act as a preservative.

Gelatin is a tasteless, odorless pure protein setting agent. When adding to another substance, both must be the same temperature i.e. add hot gelatin to hot dishes, cold to cold.

To keep fish in the refrigerator, wrap loosely in plastic wrap.

Do not wash fish. Leave it to stand in its own juices.

Smelling fish is the best guide to whether or not it is fresh.

A fish is cooked when it is white in color and a fin or gill can be easily broken away.

When baking fish, leave the skin on to hold the shape.

Remove the skin of fish when stir frying to absorb flavors.

Fish should be seasoned well, as it can be a bland food.

Bake fish ten minutes per pound. Sauté fish one minute either side. Do not overcook.

Fish can be marinated up to 24 hours in the refrigerator.

Chicken can be marinated up to two days in the refrigerator.

It is a good idea to crumb a fish fillet or chicken breast to protect the delicate meat.

When crumbing, add flavors to the egg white – dill, lemon juice, coriander.

Crumbs will stick better if done in advance and rested in the refrigerator for two hours before dry frying.

Use a metal spoon for folding egg whites into recipes. Wood or plastic will absorb the air.

Take fresh plums or apricots to a picnic, or put them in a child's lunchbox, in an egg carton lined with plastic wrap. Then they won't squash.

To make croutons for soup, place bread squares in an oven and dry bake until golden or, before baking, try spreading lightly with yogurt, crushed garlic and ricotta cheese.

To scale fish easily, first dip fish in hot water for a few minutes.

Why not cook the whole packet of brown rice? It keeps well in the refrigerator in an airtight container and it will be a great time saver.

Cook a few of the pea pods with the peas to preserve the deep green color.

To skin a tomato quickly, hold it over a naked flame until the skin bursts, turning it frequently. The skin will peel off easily and the tomato will not be soggy.

When cooking rice, add half a lemon to the water. This prevents rice sticking to the bottom of the pan.

Wash strawberries before removing stems. This avoids loss of juice.

Homemade breads will keep fresh and moist if wrapped in foil and placed in a plastic bag.

To avoid diluting the punch too much, use fruit juices for ice blocks or, for an interesting effect, add a piece of fruit such as a strawberry, cherry, a piece of pineapple, to each ice cube before adding fruit juice.

A gradual change to a new diet is recommended ... this will allow your digestive system to appreciate the changeover without too much wind.

Always keep this recipe book at the front of your collection of recipe books, and when looking for a recipe for whatever occasion, always refer to it first, before being tempted to go any further.

Think of the food you are eating. Eat slowly. Chew all food well.

When eating out at a friend's home, either eat before going and then nibble on foods allowed, or take your own meal with you. Better still, give your friend a copy of this cookbook.

Always have a pot of soup brewing on the stove, or keep a container of soup in the fridge ready to heat. When feeling hungry or thirsty, remember that soup is an excellent beverage or can be a meal on its own.

Lunches and dinners should always feature a large mixed salad of lettuce and other vegetables, cooked or raw. This will never become boring if you explore all the salad and vegetable combinations I offer you and experiment with some of your own according to your own personal taste. Salads are an important part of this diet. To enhance the salad ingredients with a dressing, they should be lightly washed and dried. A salad shaker/dryer would be an excellent asset.

Eat plenty of wholegrain breads at mealtimes. Serve hot with ricotta cheese and garlic, or slice thickly for sandwiches.

Emphasize the vegetable content of a meal, rather than the meat. Use meat to flavor a dish rather than be the dish itself. Wholemeal spaghetti, pasta and rice dishes permit minimum quantities of meat to be used and are an excellent source of natural high fiber.

Steam vegetables over a low heat to retain their full flavor and nourishment. Balance the green and yellow vegetables with at least one or two carbohydrate vegetables such as potato or rice.

Use fruit juices and herbs to flavor a dish where you would have normally used salt, sugar or other additives. You will enjoy using herbs in your cooking once you develop a taste for them after much experimenting.

Measure out a quantity of meat before cooking it, making sure you allow the correct amount for each person (approx 4 ounces per person per day). Meats can be cooked then chilled so the congealed fat may be removed and the meat then reheated, or the meat can be cooked separately from the vegetables and spread on kitchen paper to absorb the fat before using.

In recipes calling for eggs, use the whites only, as the yolks are high in cholesterol and fat. To make up the volume, mix with skimmed milk (about 2 tablespoons) or use double the amount of egg whites.

To sweeten a dish, use grated apple, apple juice, orange juice, pineapple juice (all unsweetened), mashed banana, other fruits or apple juice concentrate.

At all times choose fresh foods when available. If buying canned foods, make sure there are no preservatives or colorings, no added sugar or salt.

Invest in a food processor to save you precious time in the preparation of vegetables, fruits, nuts, meat, bread-crumbs and herbs.

Make refreshing drinks from vegetables and fruits with the aid of a juice extractor.

Keep a number of air tight containers and crispers on hand as this will allow you to store an abundance of prepared food fresh and ready to eat in the fridge or on the shelves.

EGG YOLKS –
WHAT TO DO WITH THEM

Worried about throwing out all those egg yolks? Now you don't have to – and please, your dog and cat do not deserve the high fat and cholesterol diet you are doing so well without.

EGG YOLK FACIAL

4 egg yolks
1/4 grated carrot
4 egg yolks
1/4 cup wheatgerm
4 egg yolks
2 tablespoons lemon juice
4 egg yolks
1/4 cup yogurt (non-fat)

Combine ingredients. Wash face with warm water twice. Wear scarf or shower cap, to keep hair away from your face. Lie down. Place towel over your chest and under chin. Using a pastry brush, apply mixture to face, avoiding eyes, nostrils and mouth. Leave on for at least 20 minutes. Wash off with lukewarm water. Wash again with warm water, then splash face with cold water – a great feeling.

EGG YOLK HAIR CONDITIONER

For oily hair
2 egg yolks
1/4 cup lemon juice

For dry-normal hair
3 egg yolks
1/4 cup water

Wash hair with shampoo and rinse. Combine ingredients. Massage into scalp and to the ends of your hair. Rinse twice. Now you have squeaky clean hair!

17

MEASUREMENTS AND OVEN TEMPERATURES

1 cup = 8 fl oz

Slow oven	300–350°F
Moderate oven	350–375°F
Hot oven	400°F
Very hot oven	425–450°F

CONVERSIONS AND SUBSTITUTES

$1/4$ teaspoon dried herbs - 2 tablespoons fresh herbs

2 cloves fresh garlic crushed = 1 teaspoon powdered garlic

4 teaspoons dry yeast = 10 ounces fresh yeast

1 cup carob powder = $3/4$ cup cocoa powder

$2^{1/2}$ medium sized lemons = $1/2$ cup lemon juice

1 medium sized onion = approximately 3 ounces

1 teaspoon agar powder will set approximately $1^{1/4}$–2 cups of liquid, depending on setting consistency required

1 x 10 inch agar bar will set approximately 3 cups of liquid

1 cup uncooked brown rice = nearly 3 cups cooked brown rice

2 cups uncooked soyaroni noodles = 3 cups cooked noodles

1 cup skim milk powder = 4 cups liquid milk

1 cup wholemeal flour = approximately 5 ounces

1 cup rolled oats = approximately 5 ounces

1 cup whole almonds = approximately 5 ounces

COOKING TERMS

Lightly grease: If greasing is necessary, use a good quality cold pressed oil (olive oil). Lightly wipe over the surface of the cookware and wipe off any excess using a tissue. This technique will protect the surface of the cookware and food will not stick. Most cookware will not need to be washed. Wipe over with oil while still hot and remove any small particles of food.

Diced: Use a sharp knife to cut food into small squares.

Shred: This applies to leafy vegetables. Roll leaves up tightly and cut thinly or thickly in a straight line to the end of leaves.

Segmenting fruit: Use a sharp knife. Place the fruit upright on a board and pare off the peel and pith in even slices. Cut the segments out individually after the fruit has been peeled and all traces of white pith have been removed.

Testing a cake: Insert a fine skewer or thin piece of straw from a broom into the center of the cake. If it comes out dry, the cake is cooked.

Julienne: Julienne strips are matchstick thin pieces of vegetables or fruits such as carrot, zucchini or apple.

Crudités: These are small pieces of vegetable to nibble on, or to use with dips.

Purée: Place food through a fine sieve or food processor until all food is smooth.

Serves: It is difficult to determine how much each person in the family will eat. This book has based the serves per recipe on an 'average' appetite.

Blanche: Place food quickly into boiling water, leave for just a few minutes, depending on what the food is, then remove. Plunge into iced water for a few moments to cool completely, then drain. Blanching helps retain crispness.

Simmer: Cook on low heat. Bring food to boil, turn heat down, cover and simmer for the required time. The liquid content of the food should be only just bubbling.

Steam: Place food on a rack above boiling water. The steam penetrates and cooks the food, but water does not come into contact with it. Hence, nutrients that would normally be washed away in the cooking liquid are retained.

Stir fry: Stir frying without oil or stock can only be successfully achieved if a non-stick surface is used. The surface should be very hot before you add the food. When you add the food it should be continuously stirred for a short period of time. Liquids can then be added. This method is mainly used in Chinese cooking.

KITCHEN EQUIPMENT

Food processor: This will undoubtedly be your most expensive piece of kitchen equipment. It is not an essential kitchen helper, but it will greatly reduce the time taken in the kitchen for preparation of food.

Its uses include chopping, slicing, mixing and grating ingredients for soups, casseroles, lasagne, pie crusts, slices and cakes. It is also useful for mincing meat, fish and chicken, and fresh herbs.

For all recipes using a food processor in this book, I have used a food processor with a large motor and a large capacity bowl.

Food blender: Most things can be blended in a food processor, so this is an optional extra. However, the milk and yogurt drinks and the whipped cream are blended more smoothly and more effectively in a blender. The rotary action of the blender is much faster than the processor.

Garlic press: This is useful for crushing garlic and fresh ginger to obtain juice.

Sharp knives: Blunt knives rather than sharp ones are more likely to cause accidents in the kitchen. Use cleavers or large bladed knives for chopping. Serrated knives can be used for cutting bread, citrus fruits and slicing tomatoes or other soft foods. Use small knives for peeling and slicing small foods.

Orange rinder tool: This tool readily removes the orange zest in fine strips from the orange without the pith.

Cheese grater: A small, very fine grater is excellent for making the zest of fruit into a pulp, which adds extra flavor to food.

Non-stick cookware: When not using fat or oil to cook in, it is necessary to use a non-stick surface so that food does not adhere to the surface of the cookware.

Non-scratch cooking utensils: Non-stick cookware is easily scratched and the surfaces destroyed. Do not use metal utensils on non-stick cookware. Only heavy duty plastic ones or those especially designed for this type of cookware will do.

Steamer: Steaming food helps to retain the nutrient value. You can buy steaming racks to place in pans or a steamer pan set, in which one pan sits on top of another.

Metal spoons: When folding egg whites into other ingredients always use a metal spoon. A wooden spoon absorbs the air from the egg white.

Cutting boards: you will need one small board for garlic and onions, one for fresh herbs, one for chopping meat, and another large board for everything else. Do not wash wooden chopping boards in soapy water. Gently wipe over with warm water and lightly oil the board with a cold compressed olive oil. Wipe excess oil from the board with tissues.

Vegetable scrubbing brush: Vegetables like potatoes, carrots and parsnips only need to be scrubbed clean, not peeled. Most of the nutrient value lies just below the surface of the peel. Peeling, in many instances, removes the value of the vegetable.

Chinese wok: The Chinese method of cooking is the best way to present nutritious vegetables. Only a small amount of cooking time is required and vegetables retain their color and crispness as well as their nutrient value. I use a wok with a non-stick surface. To protect your wok, never use hot soapy water to clean it. After cooking, wipe out with warm water to remove small particles of cooked food. Wipe over completely with cold pressed olive oil to remove all remaining food particles. Wipe off excess oil with tissues.

Juice extractor
Set of measuring cups and spoons
Rolling pin
Flour sifter
Wooden spoons
Metal bowls (especially for mixing egg whites)

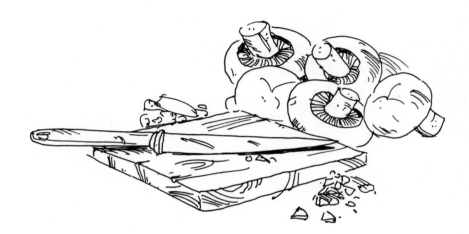

LIGHT AND EASY

ASPARAGUS ROLL UPS

Makes 10

1 cup asparagus purée (Lightly steam
fresh asparagus until tender. Drain.
Squeeze over lemon juice. Purée
and chill)
10 slices wholemeal bread, crusts
removed
1/2 cup non-fat cottage cheese
5 tablespoons fresh, finely chopped
tarragon (optional)

Using a wooden rolling pin roll out slices of bread
until they are very thin. Refrigerate for 30 minutes or
longer. Push cottage cheese through a fine sieve.
Spread bread slices with cottage cheese then with
asparagus and sprinkle over tarragon. Roll up and
secure with a small toothpick. Repeat to make 10.

Refrigerate for at least 1 hour, remove toothpick
before serving.

BROWN RICE STUFFED TOMATOES

Serves 8

8 medium tomatoes
1 cup brown rice, cooked
1 onion, finely chopped
2/3 cup currants
3 tablespoons pinenuts or almonds,
chopped
3 tablespoons chopped mint
black pepper to taste
1/2 cup wholemeal breadcrumbs

Slice tops from tomatoes and scoop out pulp with a
metal spoon. Combine rice, onion, currants, pinenuts *or* almonds, mint, tomato pulp in a pan and
season with black pepper. Bring mixture to a gentle
simmer and simmer for 1 minute. Place tomato cases
on a foil lined baking tray. Spoon mixture into the
tomatoes. Sprinkle breadcrumbs over each tomato.
Bake in a moderate oven for 20 minutes or until
breadcrumbs are browned.

Serve on a bed of rice.

CARROT WHEELS

Makes 24

6 slices wholemeal bread
1/2 cup tomato relish
1 1/2 cups finely grated carrot

Remove crusts from bread. Using a rolling pin roll out bread as thinly as possible. Lightly spread each piece of bread with tomato relish. Top with grated carrot. Roll up very tightly. Wrap securely in foil. Refrigerate overnight.

Unwrap carefully and cut each roll into 4 wheels (use a very sharp knife or an electric knife).

Place on a serving platter.

CURRIED EGGS

Makes 12

6 hard boiled eggs
1 cup cold mashed potato
1/2 teaspoon turmeric
1 teaspoon curry powder
1 cup cold puréed cooked peas

Shell eggs. Using a sharp knife carefully cut eggs in half and remove egg yolk. Place egg white on a serving platter. Combine potato, turmeric and curry powder. Mix well. Spoon curried potato mixture into half of the egg white. Spoon puréed pea mixture into the other half. Using the top end of a spoon, just move pea mixture slightly into the potato mixture to create a swirling effect. Chill before serving.

MARINATED FRUIT KABOBS

This is a refreshing way to start a main meal on a hot summer's day. Use wooden kebab sticks, approximately 4" long. Thread on bite size pieces of fruit (about 2 to 4 variations on each stick).

Suggestions
Cantaloupe ball, pineapple, apple, orange, honeydew melon ball, green grape, pear, peach, nectarine, watermelon ball, strawberry, purple grape, kiwi fruit.

Lie the kabobs in a shallow dish and pour over vinaigrette of your choice. Leave to marinate in the refrigerator until ready to serve. Serve 2 or 3 on a bed of lettuce leaves or cut a grapefruit or melon in half and stick kabobs into it.

POPPY SEED LOG

1/2 lb non-fat cottage cheese
1 tablespoon finely chopped sage
3 tablespoons finely chopped chives
1 tablespoon finely chopped parsley
1/2 cup poppy seeds

Press cottage cheese through a fine sieve, add herbs and form into a log shape. Tear off a sheet of foil, and place poppy seeds on it. Roll the log backwards and forwards through the poppy seeds to coat it thoroughly. Refrigerate for at least 2 hours, wrapped in foil.

Serve with celery sticks, carrot crackers and bunches of green and purple grapes.

PRUNE BUTTONS

Makes 24

24 prunes, pitted
1/4 cup non-fat cottage cheese
1/2 cup mashed potato
approximately 10 water chestnuts
1/4 teaspoon almond extract
sprigs of fresh dill

Combine cottage cheese, potato, water chestnuts and almond extract in a food processor and blend until smooth. Spoon into a piping bag. Pipe a small amount on each prune. Refrigerate prior to serving. Serve on a platter with a small sprig of dill on top of each prune.

SNOW PEA PODS

Approximately 30 snow peas

Filling
1 cup non-fat cottage cheese
2 tablespoons tomato relish (see page 134)
4 colossal prawns, shelled and finely chopped
2 tablespoons chopped chives
1/2 cup alfalfa sprouts

Wash, string and carefully split the snow peas. Blanch in boiling water for approximately 20 seconds. Remove, and drain. Plunge into chilled water and drain thoroughly. Combine cottage cheese, tomato relish, chopped prawns and chives. Lightly mix. Spoon mixture carefully into the snow pea pods. Press alfalfa sprouts on top of each snow pea pod.

Place on a serving platter, cover and refrigerate for at least 1 hour.

STUFFED MUSHROOMS

36 mushrooms
1 cup mashed potato
1/4 cup chopped fresh herbs (oregano,
    chives, parsley)
1/4 cup finely chopped green onions
2 tablespoons finely grated low fat
    grating cheese
1 cup wholemeal breadcrumbs

Wash mushrooms thoroughly and remove stems. Combine potato, herbs, green onions and cheese and mix well. Spoon mixture onto mushrooms and sprinkle over breadcrumbs. Bake in a hot oven 5 to 8 minutes, or place under a hot grill to brown the top.

TRIANGLE PUFFS

Makes 16

8 sheets wholemeal filo pastry
1 cup (firmly packed) grated carrot
2 medium potatoes, grated and
    drained
1/4 cup green beans/peas (chop the
    beans finely)
1/4 cup bell pepper, finely chopped
1/2 medium onion, diced
1/2 cup curry sauce (see page 55) or
    2 teaspoons fresh ginger juice
    (press ginger in a garlic crusher)
1–2 cloves garlic, crushed
1/2 cup non-fat yogurt
Combine the last 3 ingredients and
    mix well

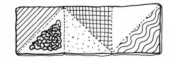

Lay two sheets of pastry one on top of the other. Using a sharp knife or scissors cut the pastry lengthwise into 4 equal strips. This will give you 16 pieces. Combine all ingredients and mix thoroughly. To make triangles place a rectangle of 2 sheets of filo on a flat bench. Fold one corner over to form the first triangle. Open back and place a spoonful of filling.

Following the diagram, fold the shaded area over the filling. Turn this over onto the spotted area. Turn over onto the check area, then onto the white area and finally onto the wavy area. The filling will now be completely concealed. Place on a lightly greased non-stick baking tray. Repeat with remaining mixture. Bake at 400°F for 15 minutes. Turn over and cook for a further 15 minutes.

Note: If wholemeal filo pastry is not available, use plain filo pastry and sprinkle oat bran or wheat bran between layers of pastry.

SALMON DIP

2 cups drained salmon
1/2 pound cottage cheese
4 tablespoons tomato paste
1 1/2 tablespoons lemon juice
black pepper to taste
3 shallots, very finely chopped

Blend all ingredients except shallots. Stir through shallots, cover and chill well before serving with a platter of vegetables.

CARROT DIP

1 bunch baby carrots
lemon juice or unsweetened orange
  juice diluted with water
1 teaspoon nutmeg
1 cup cottage cheese

Cook cleaned and chopped carrots in equal parts water and lemon juice or unsweetened orange juice diluted with water (enough liquid just to cover carrots). Simmer gently until carrots are tender. Purée the carrots, adding a squeeze of lemon juice, 1 teaspoon nutmeg and 1 cup cottage cheese. Spoon into a bowl, Refrigerate until well chilled. Serve with vegetable sticks, celery sticks or salt-free wholewheat crackers.

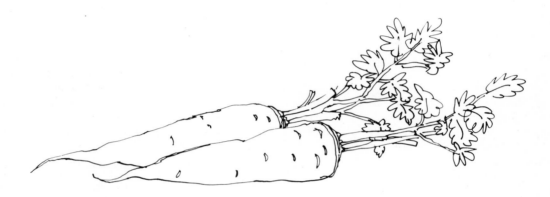

ONION DIP

Make just prior to serving

1/2 cup non-fat cottage cheese
1/2 cup non-fat yogurt
1 large odorless onion, finely
  chopped
1 green apple, peeled and grated
1 tablespoon lemon juice
cayenne pepper to taste

Combine cottage cheese and yogurt, and fold the onion through. Pour lemon juice over apple, and add to the onion mixture. Add cayenne pepper to taste.

TOMATO DIP

1 cup tomato relish (see page 134)
1 cup cooked apple purée

Combine ingredients.

SPINACH DIP

1 cup cooked puréed spinach
1/2–1 cup non-fat cottage cheese
2 teaspoons dijon mustard
1/4 cup very finely chopped bell
  pepper
1 tablespoon chopped fresh dill
dash of cayenne pepper
1 tablespoon non-fat natural yogurt
  (optional)

Push cottage cheese through a fine sieve. Add all other ingredients and mix well. If mixture is too dry, add 1 tablespoon of non-fat natural yogurt and blend through.

VEGETABLE PLATTER AND DIPS

You will need a serving platter and a selection of suitable vegetables, chosen from the following:

button mushrooms (wash
  thoroughly)
radishes, halved
green and red bell pepper strips
celery, cut into 2 inch chunks
carrots, cut in julienne strips or if
  carrots are large, cut into thin
  rounds to make crackers
snow peas, top, tail and string
cucumber, peel, cut in half
  lengthwise and scoop out seeds.
  Cut into 1 1/2 inch lengths
cherry tomatoes
cauliflower/broccoli flowerettes, drop
  into boiling water for 3 minutes;
  drain; plunge into chilled water;
  drain
zucchini strips, drop into boiling
  water for 1 minute; drain; plunge
  into chilled water; drain

Soak cauliflower, broccoli and zucchini in white wine vinegar. Drain prior to serving.
  Serve with dips.

AVOCADO DIP

Make just prior to serving so the avocado does not discolor

1 avocado (keep refrigerated until needed)
3 teaspoons lemon juice
1/2–1 cup non-fat cottage cheese
1 1/2 tablespoons unsweetened orange juice
1 teaspoon curry powder or
1/4 teaspoon cumin and 1/4 teaspoon ginger powder
3 tablespoons chopped chives

Push cottage cheese through a fine sieve. Remove avocado flesh from skin and pit. Mash with a fork. Add lemon juice. Combine all ingredients and mix well.

STOCKS AND BROTHS

BASIC CHICKEN STOCK

Makes 6¹/₂ cups

8¹/₂ cups water
any chicken bones, carcass or fresh
    meat
¹/₂ lemon
celery leaves
black pepper

Bring to a boil. Simmer for 1 hour and strain. Store in the refrigerator. Can be frozen.

CHINESE CHICKEN STOCK

4¹/₂ pounds chicken with skin and
    visible fat removed
¹/₂ lemon
1 onion
1 x 1 inch piece ginger root, peeled
4¹/₂ cups of water (add more if
    using larger chicken)
1 cup unsweetened orange juice

Place all ingredients in a large pan. Chicken should be just covered with liquid. Bring to a boil, reduce heat and simmer for 1 hour. Remove chicken and cover with cold water until completely cold. This retains moisture and makes the chicken succulent. Strain. Cool stock, refrigerate and remove the fat. Stock is ready to use. Chicken meat can be used in the bits and pieces bowl or sliced for sandwiches.

BEEF STOCK

Makes 8¹/₂ cups

4¹/₂ pounds beef bones
1 onion
2 bay leaves
2 stalks celery with leafy tops
1 medium carrot
6 black peppercorns (optional)
8¹/₂ cups water

Remove all visible fat from beef bones. Put all the above ingredients in a large pan. Bring to the boil. Turn heat down to lowest setting. Leave to simmer for a least 3 hours. Remove from heat. Strain. Leave to cool and refrigerate. Remove congealed fat, which will set on top of stock, before using.

Use as required for flavoring soups. This stock can be kept in the refrigerator or frozen.

FISH STOCK

Makes 8¹/₂ cups

4¹/₂ pounds clean fish heads or
*   bones*
6¹/₂ cups water
2¹/₂ cups apple juice or dry white
*   wine*
2 large white onions or equivalent in
*   leeks*
2 carrots, tops removed and peeled
¹/₂ cup parsley heads
3 bay leaves
1 sprig of fresh thyme or marjoram
¹/₂ lemon

Peel and chop onions. Place all ingredients in a large pan and bring to a boil. Simmer for 30 minutes. Strain. Pour strained liquid through a fine piece of cheesecloth or handkerchief.

Use as required to add flavor to fish-based soups or casseroles.

VEGETABLE STOCK

potatoes
carrots
onions
celery stalks
celery leaves
spinach
rutabaga
turnip
parsnip
tomatoes

Could also add
1/2 lemon
black pepper
1/4 cup dry sherry
1/4 cup orange juice
1/4 cup tomato juice

All or any of these vegetables in a combination would be suitable to make a vegetable stock. Chop the vegetables and cover them with water and add any extras. Bring to a boil and simmer for 20 minutes. Cover and leave to stand. When cold, strain. Purée the vegetable pulp and set aside. (This could be used to thicken soups.) The strained stock can be kept in the refrigerator and used as a base for soup as required.

Soups

I look forward to the warmth of winter fires, knowing it is that time of the year for stockpots of soup brewing in my kitchen.

I hardly ever cook the same soup twice – the soup of the day depends on the stock on hand, and what vegetables or fruits are ready to be picked fresh from the garden.

There is enjoyment in a chilled summer soup, on a hot summer's day – but nothing near the pleasures that the warmth of a hot soup on a cold day brings!

Soup is a liquid food, full of goodness, made from meat and vegetable stocks and sometimes still containing small amounts of fat-free meat, and sometimes all the vegetables. The importance of the soup is that it is all goodness, it is very easily digested and may be drunk or eaten at any time of the day. In early times, monks in the monasteries would always have a stockpot on the fire for weary travellers.

I have served a soup with the same ingredients more than once, but because the ingredients have been grated, or sometimes finely chopped, or perhaps puréed I have created an entirely different effect and sometimes flavor.

Begin with a basic soup idea, for example, tomato soup, vary one ingredient at a time and then perhaps two to create a different taste result.

Your presentation is also important. It can make a basic soup an artistic and visual delight. Serve soup in pottery mugs for those casual times, in a bowl or serve the soup from a tureen at the dinner table – an interesting way to create conversation at the table as the bowls circulate with their delightful aromas.

ASPARAGUS SOUP

Serves 4–6

3 cups chicken stock (see page 31)
1 cup finely chopped celery leaves
3 large potatoes, peeled and chopped
3/4 pound cooked asparagus
1/2 cup asparagus cooking liquid
1 tablespoon lemon juice

Combine the first 3 ingredients and cook until potatoes are tender. Add remaining ingredients and purée. Return to heat. Heat through and serve.

CARROT AND ORANGE SOUP

Serves 6

12 medium sized baby carrots,
  grated
1 large onion, diced
3 cups chicken stock (see page 31)
2 cups orange juice
1 tablespoon finely grated orange
  rind
1 tablespoon finely grated lemon
  rind
ground black pepper to taste
  (optional)
natural non-fat yogurt and chopped
  chives

Place carrots, onion and chicken stock in a pan. Bring to a boil and simmer covered for 20 minutes. Add orange juice, orange and lemon rind, and ground black pepper to taste. Simmer for a further 10 minutes and stir occasionally.

This soup can be served hot or cold. Serve with a heaped teaspoon of yogurt and chives to each soup bowl.

Variation For a thicker soup add 2 potatoes, peeled and cut into small cubes with carrots, onions and chicken stock. Purée the soup in a blender.

CHILLED SUMMER BEET SOUP

Serves 6–8

4 cups puréed cooked beet
4 cups beef stock (see page 32)
2–4 tablespoons finely chopped
  garlic chives
2 teaspoons finely grated lemon rind
ground black pepper to taste
  (optional)

Combine all ingredients and mix well. Chill. To serve, garnish with a green onion and grated raw beet.

CARROT AND TURNIP SOUP WITH CORIANDER

Serves 4–6

1/2 pound baby carrots
1/2 pound turnips
4 1/2 cups chicken stock (see page 31)
black pepper
2 tablespoons non-fat yogurt
2 teaspoons ground coriander
1 teaspoon ground cumin
1 tbsp finely chopped coriander
    leaves

Clean and slice the carrots and turnips. Cook the carrots and turnips in 1/4 cup of stock for approximately 6 minutes, stirring now and then. Heat the stock and pour it on to the vegetables. Bring to the boil and add pepper to taste and simmer for 30 minutes covered. Purée in a food processor or blender and return to a clean pan. Reheat and add yogurt and more pepper if necessary. Add the spices and the chopped coriander leaves, mix well and stand for 5 minutes before serving.

FISH SOUP

Serves 6–8

2 small leeks (or 2 medium onions if
    leeks are not available)
2–3 cloves garlic
1/2 cup unsweetened orange juice
1 pound ripe tomatoes, skinned,
    seeds removed and chopped
2 level tablespoons tomato paste
freshly ground black pepper
    (optional)
8 1/2 cups fish stock (see page 32)
1 tablespoon chopped fresh basil
1 small carrot cut into julienne
    strips
1/2 cup leeks (white part only), cut
    into julienne strips
1/2 cup celery, cut into julienne strips
1/3 cup fennel, cut into julienne
    strips (optional)
2 pounds white fish cut into small
    strips
8 scallops, cleaned (optional)
1/4 cup finely chopped fresh parsley

Remove the green leaves from leeks and discard. Rinse leeks under running water to remove dirt. Slice leeks thinly.

Add leeks, garlic and orange juice to a pan and cook over a gentle heat for 5 to 10 minutes or until all juice is absorbed. Add tomatoes and tomato paste. Season with black pepper if desired. Cook a further 5 minutes. Add strained fish stock, basil, carrot, leeks, celery and fennel. Bring to a boil and simmer for 10 minutes with the lid on. Add fish and simmer for a further 5 minutes with the lid on. Add scallops and simmer 4 minutes more.

Serve immediately in a large soup tureen with chopped parsley and hot crispy wholemeal bread.

Note: If you are using scallops, add them and simer 4 minutes more.

CURRIED VEGETABLE SOUP

Serves 6–8

3 cups beef stock (see page 32)
1 inch piece of fresh ginger, peeled
 and crushed
1 teaspoon curry powder
6 ounces leeks, roughly chopped
4 ounces parsnip, diced
1/2 pound pumpkin, peeled and
 cubed
1 zucchini, chopped into rounds
12 oz can salt free tomatoes and
 juice
1 cup water

Combine all ingredients in a large pan and simmer for 3 hours. Stir occasionally so vegetables do not stick to the bottom of pan.

CORN AND VEGETABLE CHOWDER

Serves 8

3 cloves garlic, crushed
1 inch piece of fresh ginger, finely
 chopped
6 ounces leeks, finely chopped
2 cups water
6 ounces celery, finely chopped
1 medium parsnip, diced
1 large carrot, chopped
4 potatoes, peeled and cut into small
 cubes
1 1/2 pounds pumpkin, finely chopped
2 zucchini, cut into small rounds
2 corn cobs
10 green beans, cut into 1 1/2 inch
 lengths
9 cups water or vegetable stock (see
 page 33)
ground black pepper to taste
 (optional)

Cook garlic, ginger and leeks in 2 cups of water in a large pan for 10 minutes. Add all other ingredients. Simmer for 2 hours. Remove corn cobs and cut away corn kernels. Return corn kernels to the soup. Stir through. Adjust flavor by adding more ground black pepper if desired.

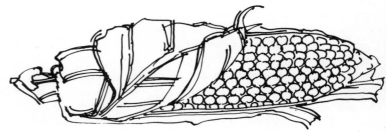

HEARTY VEGETABLE SOUP

Serves 8

8¹/₂ cups chicken stock (see page 31)
8 ounces leeks, finely chopped
1 cup chopped celery
1 cup chopped green beans
1 cup shelled peas
2 cups chopped carrot
1 cup chopped zucchini
1 cup chopped parsnip
¹/₄ cup cracked wheat (bulgur)
1 cup water
1 teaspoon dried marjoram

Combine all ingredients in a large pan. Simmer for 2 hours. Stir occasionally so vegetables do not stick to the bottom of the pan. This soup is almost a meal.

CELERY SOUP

Serves 4

4 cups vegetable or chicken stock
  (see page 31)
5 ounces chopped leeks
1 pound celery (preferably leaves
  and top half of a bunch of celery)
2 potatoes, peeled and chopped
piece of fresh ginger, chopped finely
1 tablespoon lemon juice
rind of 1 lemon, finely grated
1 cup water
1 cup finely sliced celery

Combine all ingredients (except the cup of finely sliced celery) in a large pan. Simmer for 1¹/₂ hours. Purée. Return soup to a clean pan. Add the cup of finely sliced celery and stir through. Reheat and serve.

MELON SOUP

Serves 6

4 cups chicken stock (see page 31)
1 teaspoon fresh crushed ginger
1 tablespoon dry sherry
1 cantaloupe, peeled, seeded and
  grated

Place the first 3 ingredients in a pan and bring to a boil. Turn heat down and gently simmer for 8 minutes. Remove from heat and add cantaloupe. Refrigerate. Before serving, adjust flavorings by adding the following:

- 2 teaspoons finely grated lemon or orange rind
- 2 tablespoons finely chopped parsley or mint
- 2 tablespoons finely chopped shallots

39

IT'S A BEAN BREW

Serves 6–8

2 cups mixed beans (including red
   kidney, split peas, lentils, baby
   lima, garbanzo)
8 cups of stock (of your own choice)
1 large leek
2 cloves garlic, crushed
1/2 cup unsweetened orange juice
1 cup fresh chopped tomatoes, peeled
   and seeded
1/2 cup chopped celery leaves
1/2 cup grated parsnip
1/2 cup grated carrot
1/2 cup finely chopped parsley
1/2 teaspoon dried basil
1/2 teaspoon dried oregano
1/2 teaspoon dried rosemary
fresh ground black pepper to taste
   (optional)

Rinse and soak the beans overnight or pour boiling water over them to cover, place the lid on and leave for 2 hours. Drain. Split the leek in half and wash thoroughly (white and green part) and chop thinly. Cook leek and garlic in the orange juice over a gentle heat until soft and transparent. Add the tomatoes and cook a further 3 to 4 minutes. Add all the other ingredients and simmer with the lid on for 2 hours or until beans are soft. Stir occasionally, so that beans do not stick to the bottom of the pan.

MY MINESTRONE

Serves 4–6

2 garlic cloves
1 large onion
9 cups vegetable or chicken stock
   (see page 31)
2 large carrots
3 sticks celery and leaves
1 large potato
3 small zucchini
10 green beans
1/2 cup sliced mushrooms
2 x 1 pound cans tomatoes
3 cups cooked haricot beans
1/2 cup cooked brown rice or 1/2 cup
   wholemeal macaroni
black pepper
1 teaspoon marjoram
any leftover chicken meat could also
   be added

Crush garlic and chop onions. Cook for 6 minutes in 1/2 cup stock. Add remaining stock and vegetables, then tomatoes. Season with black pepper. Bring to a boil and simmer for 1 hour, stirring occasionally. Purée 2 cups of soup in a blender and return this to the soup. Add beans, rice or macaroni and marjoram and heat through for further 5 minutes.

POTATO CURRY SOUP

Serves 4–6

6 large potatoes
2 leeks
2 medium onions
¼ cup unsweetened orange juice
6 cups chicken stock (see page 31)
1 teaspoon curry powder (or more if
  desired)
½ teaspoon ginger
1 bay leaf
3 tablespoons chopped parsley

Peel potatoes and cut into cubes. Wash leeks thoroughly and cut in half lengthwise, chop thinly. Peel and chop onions finely. Cook onions and leeks in the orange juice over a gentle heat, until they are quite soft and transparent. Add potatoes and cook for a further 3 minutes, tossing them through the onions gently.

Add the stock, curry powder, ginger and bay leaf. Cover and simmer for 30 minutes or until potatoes are soft. Purée. Stir through parsley before serving.

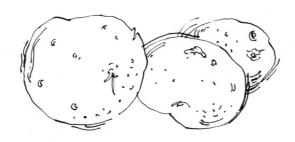

PUMPKIN AND PARSNIP SOUP

Serves 8

6 cups chicken stock (see page 31)
4 cups water
2 pounds finely minced pumpkin
  (done in a food processor)
6 ounces parsnip finely minced
  (done in a food processor)
12 ounces celery stalks and leaves,
  finely sliced
ground black pepper to taste
  (optional)
pinch of nutmeg
2 cups green onions, chopped, for
  garnish

Combine all ingredients except garnish in a large pan. Bring to a boil. Turn heat down to a simmer. Cook for 2 hours. Stir occasionally.

Before serving, add 2 cups chopped green onions. Serve immediately.

PUMPKIN SOUP

Serves 6–8

1½ pounds pumpkin, peeled and
   finely diced
4 cups defatted chicken stock (see
   page 31)
or
2 cups unsweetened orange juice
   and 2 cups water
1 medium sized onion
1 teaspoon fresh ginger, finely
   chopped
1 clove garlic, crushed (optional)
¼ cup salt free tomato paste
½ teaspoon cumin (optional)

Cook onion, ginger and garlic in 2 tablespoons water for 3 minutes or until transparent. To get the best flavor from onions without cooking in oil, always place lid on pan while onions are cooking. Add all other ingredients. Cook for 15–20 minutes or until pumpkin is tender. Purée. Serve with a thin slice of orange and garnish with parsley.

SUMMER CUCUMBER YOGURT SOUP

Serves 6

2 large cucumbers
2 cups non-fat yogurt
½ cup skim milk
2 tablespoons chives or green
   onions, finely chopped
2 teaspoons fresh dill, finely chopped
1 red apple

Peel cucumbers and cut in half. Remove seeds and grate. Combine remaining ingredients and mix well. Chill for several hours so that flavor can develop. Garnish with thin slices of apple.

ZUCCHINI SOUP

Serves 6

¾ pound grated zucchini
2 onions, finely sliced
1 carrot, finely chopped
1 potato, finely chopped
2 tablespoons unsweetened orange
   juice
3 cups chicken stock (see page 31)
1 tablespoon finely chopped fresh
   rosemary
1 tablespoon finely chopped chives

Place onions, carrot, potato and orange juice in a large pan. Cover and simmer over gentle heat for 5 minutes. Add stock, herbs and stir through the zucchini. Simmer for a further 20 minutes. Purée half the soup and stir through remaining soup. Reheat and serve.

TOMATO SOUP WITH BASIL

Serves 8

3 cloves garlic, crushed
2 medium leeks, finely chopped
1 cup finely chopped celery and
  leaves
1/4 cup vegetable stock or water (see
  page 33)
5 pounds tomatoes peeled, seeded
  and roughly chopped
1 cup vegetable stock
2 tablespoons pure tomato paste
2–3 teaspoons fresh finely chopped
  basil or 1 teaspoon dried ground
  black pepper (optional)

In a large pan, add garlic, leeks, celery and 1/4 cup vegetable stock or water. Simmer for 10 minutes. Add tomatoes and 1 cup of vegetable stock. Simmer for 20 minutes. Add tomato paste, basil and season with ground black pepper to taste. Simmer for a further 10 minutes and serve.

WINTER STOCKPOT

Serves 6–8

2 cloves garlic, crushed
1 large onion, cut into rings
2 leeks, finely sliced
1/2 cup of stock (of choice)
2 large potatoes
1 small turnip or rutabaga
2 stalks celery
1/2 small cauliflower
4 ripe tomatoes, peeled and seeded
1 cup green beans, sliced
1/2 cup peas
5 cups stock
2 teaspoons mixed fresh herbs or
  1 teaspoon dried
1/4 cup cooked wholemeal pasta
  shells or wholemeal rice
1 tablespoon finely grated lemon
  rind
ground black pepper to taste
  (optional)

Cut all vegetables into small bite-size pieces. Break cauliflower into flowerettes. Chop tomatoes. Cook garlic, onion and leeks in 1/2 cup stock until softened. Add potato, turnip or rutabaga, celery, cauliflower, tomatoes, beans, peas and stock.

Simmer for 11/2 hours. Add herbs, pasta shells or rice and stir through. Simmer for a further 15 minutes. Season with ground black pepper if desired.

TOMATO SOUP

Serves 4–6

1 medium sized onion, diced
1/2 teaspoon oregano
1/2 teaspoon basil
*2 celery stalks, including green
  foliage, diced*
2 x 12 ounce cans salt free tomatoes
2 tablespoons salt free tomato paste

Cook onion, herbs and celery in a little water until soft (approximately 3 minutes). Purée tomatoes and tomato paste until smooth. Add to the onion and cook gently for 10–15 minutes. Purée again and serve immediately.

Variations
- Add 1 cup grated raw carrot before serving
- Add 1 cup finely sliced celery before serving
- Add 1 cup finely diced mixed red and green peppers before serving
- Add 1/4 cup fresh chives, finely chopped
- Add 2 teaspoons fresh ginger juice when cooking the onion
- Add 1 cup potato, peeled, diced and cooked before serving
- Serve chilled tomato soup with non-fat yogurt and a sprinkling of fresh herbs of your choice.

VICHYSSOISE

Serves 6

4 cups chicken stock (see page 31)
*4 medium potatoes, peeled and
  chopped*
3 medium onions, chopped
3 leeks, sliced
1 tablespoon orange rind
1/2 teaspoon marjoram
2 tablespoons parsley, chopped
4 oz non-fat yogurt
black pepper to taste

Place chicken stock into a pan and bring to a boil. Add potatoes, onions, leeks, orange rind and simmer for 20 minutes. Cool a little and place in a blender. Chill well and add marjoram, parsley, yogurt and black pepper before serving.

WATERMELON SOUP

Serves 4

4¹/₂ pounds watermelon
2 cups apple juice
1 cup grated apple
1 teaspoon mixed spice (optional)
small piece of fresh ginger, crushed
grated rind of 1 lemon
natural non-fat yogurt

Peel the watermelon and reserve a small amount for garnish. Remove seeds and chop flesh roughly. Place the first 6 ingredients in a pan. Bring to a boil, stirring constantly and gently simmer for 20 minutes. Remove from heat. Press through a strainer into a clean bowl. Chill thoroughly before serving.

Serve in bowls adding a heaped teaspoon of yogurt and thinly sliced piece of watermelon to garnish.

SALADS

SPROUTS

Sprouts are vegetables high in vitamin C, a good souce of pure protein; they contain natural carbohydrates, vitamins and minerals. They grow in a jar and reach their desired length ($1/2$–2 inches) in 3 to 5 days.

You can buy commercial sprouters but a jar with a piece of cheesecloth secured over the opening is acceptable.

Choose from a wide variety of seeds, beans and lentils available. Sprout one variety or combine two or more varieties for an added interest in texture and flavor.

Soak the seeds, beans and lentils for 6 hours in lukewarm water. Drain. Leave in a light place (not direct sunlight). Rinse sprouts every day and drain well.

Eat them in salads, add to sandwiches, drop them onto soup prior to serving, use them as a garnish or juice them with other fruits and vegetables. They can be added to any cooked meals prior to serving, for example, casseroles, omelettes.

APPLE SALAD

Serves 6 approximately

2 green apples
2 red apples
1 small red bell pepper
1 small green bell pepper
2 tablespoons pinenuts, roasted
  under broiler
2 stalks celery
1/2 cup apple juice
2 tablespoons lemon juice
1 tablespoon cider vinegar
2 tablespoons fresh mint, finely
  chopped
2 tablespoons fresh chives, finely
  chopped

Core apples and cut into thin wedges. Dice bell peppers finely. Cut celery into thin slices. Mix apple juice, lemon juice and vinegar and combine with salad ingredients and pinenuts. Sprinkle with mint and chives. Serve with alfalfa sprouts.

BANANA AND CELERY SALAD

Serves 4

1 lettuce
4 bananas (not too ripe)
1/4 cup lemon juice and 1/2 cup
water, combined
3 cups celery, diagonally sliced
chopped chives
1 cup natural non-fat yogurt
black pepper

Set aside 4 crisp lettuce cups. Shred the remaining lettuce finely. Peel bananas and slice diagonally. Soak in lemon juice and water for 5 minutes. Drain and towel dry. Combine bananas, shredded lettuce and celery in a bowl. Mix chives in yogurt and add black pepper to taste. Add this mixture to the lettuce, bananas and celery and toss well. Spoon equal amounts into each lettuce leaf.

CARROT AND RAISIN SALAD

Serves 1

1/2 cup raisins
1/4 lemon or orange juice
1 1/2 cups carrot, grated or
1 cup grated carrot and 1 cup
grated apple

Dressing combine 1/2 cup non-fat yogurt, 1 tablespoon lemon juice, 1 tablespoon vinegar

Take washed seeded raisins and soak in lemon juice or orange juice. When raisins are plump, mix with grated carrot or grated carrot and grated apple. Toss through dressing and serve in lettuce cups.

HAWAIIAN COLESLAW

Serves 4–6 as a main course

4 cups green cabbage, finely
shredded
1 cup fresh pineapple chunks or
unsweetened canned pineapple
pieces
1 cup green bell pepper strips
1 cup red bell pepper strips
1/2 cup carrot, diced
1/2 cup mayonnaise (see page 56)
1/4 cup unsweetened pineapple juice

Combine all ingredients in a salad bowl. Combine mayonnaise and pineapple juice. Pour dressing over coleslaw and toss well. Chill for at least 1 hour before serving.

CUCUMBER AND COLESLAW SALAD

All ingredients should be well chilled

Serves 1

1 small cucumber
1 cup finely shredded red cabbage
1 red apple, cored and cut into
*   julienne strips*
2 tablespoons finely chopped
*   odorless onion*
1/4 teaspoon dried caraway seed
2 tablespoons mayonnaise
*   (see page 56)*
1 tablespoon roasted pinenuts (to
*   roast pinenuts, place on a non-*
*   stick baking pan over heat. Move*
*   them constantly until lightly*
*   browned.)*

Peel cucumber and cut in half lengthwise. Scoop out seeds, leaving a hollow space. Combine cabbage, apple, onion, caraway seed and mayonnaise. Toss well. Place both cucumber halves on a dinner plate. Spoon cabbage and apple mixture into the hollows and let overflow onto dinner plate.

FRUITY COLESLAW

Serves 6–8 as a main course

6 cups white cabbage, finely
*   shredded*
2 oranges, peeled and segmented
1/4 cup dried apricots, cut into thin
*   strips*
1/4 cup dried peaches, cut into thin
*   strips*
1/4 cup green onions, finely sliced
1/4 cup celery, finely sliced
1/4 cup shredded coconut (optional)
1 cup fresh pineapple or
*   unsweetened canned pineapple*
*   pieces*
2 teaspoons orange rind
2 teaspoons lemon rind
1/2–1 cup orange dressing

Combine all ingredients in a large salad bowl. Pour over orange dressing and toss well. Leave to stand for at least 1 hour before serving. Serve chilled.

Orange dressing
1 cup unsweetened orange juice
2 teaspoons cornstarch
1–2 teaspoons white wine vinegar

Combine all ingredients in a small pan. Bring to the boil, stirring until sauce thickens. Cool and refrigerate.

LOBSTER SALAD

Serves 1

1 large lettuce leaf (soak in chilled
   water so it will curl to make crisp
   cup shape)
4 slices cooked beet
3 ounces lobster
6 orange segments
3 slices honeydew melon
2 slices of kiwi fruit to garnish
2 teaspoons finely grated orange
   rind
1/4 cup orange curried sauce (see
   page 56)

Place lettuce cup on a dinner plate. Add beet slices, lobster to one side, orange segments on the other. Place melon slices alongside the lettuce cup and kiwi fruit at one end of the melon slices. Sprinkle over with the orange rind and spoon over the dressing. Serve.

CARROT, ZUCCHINI AND MUSHROOM SALAD

Serves 4

6 ounces carrot, cut in thin julienne
   strips
6 ounces zucchini, cut in thin
   julienne strips
3 ounces mushrooms, thinly sliced
1/4 cup fresh parsley, finely chopped
2 tablespoons fresh basil, finely
   chopped
2 tablespoons tarragon vinegar
1 lettuce

Blanch carrots and zucchini. Add all remaining ingredients and toss well.

ORANGE AND MINT SALAD

4 oranges
1 cucumber
1 large Spanish onion
mint leaves
white wine vinegar

Peel oranges and remove pith. Peel cucumber and run a fork down the cucumber lengthwise, all the way around to give it an attractive finish. Peel onion and slice into rings. Arrange layers of onion, cucumber then orange alternately in a bowl. Sprinkle each layer of orange with mint before repeating. Pour enough white wine vinegar over to cover. Cover with plastic wrap and chill prior to serving.

CANTALOUPE WITH SHRIMP SALAD

Serves 1

3 mignonette lettuce leaves
1/2 cantaloupe (well chilled)
3 ounces small shrimp, shelled and
*   deveined*
1/4 cup grated cucumber flesh
1/4 cup grated apple
2 tablespoons lemon juice
2 teaspoons fresh dill, finely chopped
1/2 cup red pepper strips
2 tablespoons mayonnaise and 2
*   teaspoons tomato paste, combined*
*   well.*

Remove seeds from cantaloupe and peel. Cut out a U-shape on one side of the cantaloupe, (so the filling can fall out onto the lettuce). Combine shrimp, cucumber, apple lemon juice and dill. Refrigerate for 1 hour.

Add pepper and toss through. Place the lettuce on a dinner plate. Sit cantaloupe on lettuce and spoon filling into its center. Let some filling fall out onto the lettuce. Spoon over dressing. Serve.

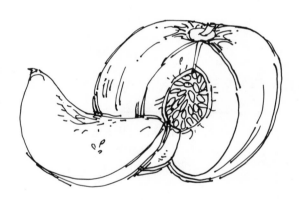

HOT POTATO SALAD

washed new potatoes
1 onion
1 green bell pepper
1 red bell pepper
celery, chopped
grated carrot
black pepper
mayonnaise
parmesan cheese

Cook potatoes in their skins until just tender. Peel potatoes and chop roughly. Finely chop onion, peppers and celery and grate carrot. Combine with potatoes and add black pepper. Pour over mayonnaise and lightly dust with cheese. Spoon into a shallow ovenproof dish and place in a hot oven for 20 minutes or until top starts to brown.

VEGETABLE PASTA SALAD

Serves 4–6

8 ounces soyaroni noodles
1/2 cup carrot, diced
1/2 cup celery, diced
1/2 cup red bell pepper, diced
1/2 cup green bell pepper, diced
1/2 cup corn
1/2 cup diced red apple
2 tablespoons parsley, finely chopped
2 tablespoons fresh chives, finely chopped
1 tablespoon tarragon vinegar
1 tablespoon unsweetened orange juice
1 teaspoon low salt soy sauce (optional)

Cook soyaroni noodles until tender. Drain well. Add all other ingredients and toss well. Refrigerate, covered.

CHICKEN HAWAII SALAD

Serves 1

3 ounces cooked chicken, broken up
1/4 cup cooked corn kernels
1/4 cup crushed unsweetened pineapple
1/4 cup green bell pepper strips
4 cauliflower flowerettes (If you don't like them raw, drop them into boiling water for 2 minutes. Drain. Plunge into chilled water. Drain.)
1/2–1 cup mung bean sprouts
4 cherry tomatoes cut in half
1/4 cup spicy tomato dressing (see page 57)

Combine all ingredients and toss through dressing. Refrigerate for at least 1 hour. Spoon into a bowl. Serve.

Opposite:
Potato curry soup (p41) Celery soup (p39)
Hearty vegetable soup (p39)

TUNA SALAD

3 lettuce leaves
1 medium tomato
1/2 cup cooked peas
2 teaspoons finely chopped mint
3 baby carrots, washed (peeled if
    necessary)
3 ounces tuna (water packed)
1/2 lemon
2 tablespoons finely chopped green
    onions
4 green bell pepper rings

Slice the top off the tomato. Scoop out the seeds and flesh. Discard. Combine peas and mint and spoon into tomato case. Refrigerate. Drop carrots into boiling water. Cook for 3 minutes. Drain. Plunge into cold water. Drain. Squeeze lemon over tuna and add onion. Place lettuce leaves on a dinner plate and position the tomato on the lettuce leaves to one side. Place carrots side by side in front and tuna at their sides on the green pepper rings.

SALMON OR TUNA COLESLAW SALAD

1/2 cup finely shredded savoy
    cabbage (crinkly leaves)
1/2 cup finely shredded red cabbage
2 tablespoons chopped green onions
1/4 cup finely sliced celery
1/4 cup crushed, unsweetened
    pineapple
3 ounces flaked salmon or tuna
    (water packed)
2 tablespoons mustard dressing

Combine all ingredients and toss well. Refrigerate for at least 2 hours before serving. Spoon into a bowl. Serve.

SPICY SPROUT SALAD

Serves approximately 12

4 celery stalks, finely sliced
5 ounces mung bean sprouts
5 ounces lentil sprouts
1 cup raisins
1 cup unsweetened orange juice
1/2–1 teaspoon cumin

Soak raisins in orange juice with cumin for at least 2 hours or overnight. Combine all ingredi-ents and mix well.

Opposite:
Fruity coleslaw (p49) Orange and mint salad (p50)
Salmon coleslaw (p53) Apple salad (p47)

53

RICE AND CORN COMBINATION SALAD

Serves 8–10

2 cups brown rice
1 cup raisins
1/2 teaspoon cumin powder
1 cup orange juice (unsweetened)
3/4 cup corn kernels
3/4 cup chopped celery
3/4 cup green peppers, chopped
3 ounces finely cut julienne carrot
1 can baby corn (wash under cold
*   water to rinse off excess salt)*
1/2 cup fresh parsley, finely chopped

Optional extra
1/2 cup almonds, cut in half

Cook rice until just tender. Drain well. Toss with all remaining ingredients. Refrigerate covered.

DRESSINGS

CREAMY COTTAGE CHEESE DRESSING

Makes approximately 1 cup

6 ounces low fat cottage cheese
1 tablespoon apple juice concentrate
1 tablespoon tarragon vinegar
1/4 cup of unsweetened apple or pineapple juice

Combine all ingredients in a blender and mix until thick and creamy. Refrigerate.

CURRY DRESSING

Makes approximately 1/2 cup

1/2 cup non-fat yogurt
1 teaspoon curry powder
1 teaspoon tomato paste (salt free)
1 tablespoon unsweetened orange juice

Mix all ingredients thoroughly and keep refrigerated.

FRENCH DRESSING

Makes approximately 1 cup

2 tablespoons fresh basil or 1 teaspoon dry
1/2 teaspoon pepper
1/3 cup fresh lemon juice
2 tablespoons fresh parsley
2 teaspoons fresh lemon rind
2/3 cup wine vinegar

Place all ingredients in a sealed jar. Shake well and store in the refrigerator.

GARLIC VINAIGRETTE

Makes approximately 1¹/₄ cups

3/4 cup apple juice
1/2 cup white wine vinegar
2 tablespoons lemon juice
2 teaspoons grated lemon rind
4 small cloves garlic, peeled and cut
   in half

Combine all ingredients in a screw top jar and keep in refrigerator. Shake every now and then. Remove garlic prior to serving, or remove and crush then return to vinaigrette.

ORANGE CURRIED SAUCE

Makes 1 cup

1 cup unsweetened orange juice
1–2 teaspoons curry powder
2 teaspoons arrowroot

Mix the arrowroot and curry powder with a small amount of the orange juice to make a paste. Stir through remaining orange juice. Place in a small pan. Slowly bring to boil until sauce thickens. Cool. Refrigerate.

Use as required. Excellent over chicken, turkey, cantaloupe, cucumber and pineapple.

MAYONNAISE

Makes 2 cups

3/4 cup low fat evaporated milk
1/4 cup apple juice concentrate
2 teaspoons dijon mustard
1/2 cup wine vinegar

Place ingredients in a screw top jar and shake well. Store in refrigerator. Shake well before each use.

MUSTARD DRESSING

Makes approximately 1 cup

1 cup non-fat yogurt
1 teaspoon dry mustard
1 tablespoon dijon mustard
1 tablespoon tarragon vinegar

Mix the dry mustard with a small amount of the yogurt to blend in thoroughly. Add this to all other ingredients. Mix well. Store in refrigerator.

HERB VINAIGRETTE

Makes approximately 1¼ cups

3/4 cup unsweetened orange juice
1/2 cup white wine vinegar
2 tablespoons finely chopped fresh
oregano
2 tablespoons finely chopped fresh
chives
2 tablespoons finely chopped fresh
parsley

Combine all ingredients and mix well. Store in refrigerator.

SPICY FRUIT DRESSING

Makes approximately ½ cup

1/2 cup non-fat yogurt
1/4 teaspoon allspice
1/4 teaspoon nutmeg
1 tablespoon unsweetened orange
juice

Combine all ingredients and mix well. Store in refrigerator.

SPICY TOMATO DRESSING

Makes approximately 2¼ cups

1 cup tomato juice (salt free)
1 cup unsweetened orange juice
rind of 1 orange, finely grated
1/4 cup white wine vinegar
2 small cloves garlic
1/2 teaspoon dried oregano
1/2 teaspoon dried basil
dash of cayenne pepper
3 teaspoons arrowroot
1 tablespoon water

Combine the first 8 ingredients in a pan and slowly bring to a boil. Mix arrowroot with the water and stir through to thicken. Simmer for 2 minutes. Leave to cool. Store in the refrigerator. Remove garlic before using.

FISH

FISH AND CHIPS

Fish
Choose low fat varieties of fish (allow
   2–3 ounces per person)
wholemeal flour
fine wholemeal breadcrumbs
1–2 egg whites
lemon juice

Squeeze lemon juice over fish. Dip fish in flour and shake off excess. Dip in lightly beaten egg white and press down in breadcrumbs until both sides are evenly coated. Shake off excess. Refrigerate fish in crumbs for at least 2 hours prior to cooking. Cook in a lightly greased non-stick pan until both sides are golden brown (approximately 3 minutes each side).
or
Place in a lightly floured oven bag, seal and cook at 400°F for 15–20 minutes.

Fish cooks quickly, so do not overcook. Fish is cooked when an inserted knife flakes the flesh easily.

To help fish retain moisture and to add flavor, fish fillets can be marinated in fruit juices with fresh herbs, garlic, ginger, tomato paste, white wine, non-fat yogurt and spices. Try your own combinations.

Place fish from marinade into breadcrumbs and cook as above.

Chips   Cut peeled or unpeeled potatoes into chips. Place on a non-stick baking tray. Cook at 500°F for 15 minutes or until browned. Non-fat yogurt can be brushed over the chips to help in the browning process.

Add flavor by sprinkling over garlic powder, onion powder, cayenne pepper or finely ground skim milk cheese with herbs.

Potatoes can be peeled and cut into chips and quickly sealed in plastic bags to freeze. Use as required and cook as above.

CHINESE SPRING ROLLS

Makes 10

1 pound shredded cabbage
1 medium sized red bell pepper,
    diced
8 green onions, finely chopped
4 ounces mushrooms, finely chopped
8 water chestnuts, diced
1 pound cooked prawns, chopped
or 1 pound cooked chicken, chopped
1 teaspoon fresh ginger, chopped
2 tablespoons dry sherry
1 tablespoon low salt soy sauce
1 tablespoon apple juice concentrate
1 tablespoon cornstarch mixed with
    1/4 cup water
2 teaspoons low salt soy sauce
2 tablespoons water
20 sheets of wholemeal filo pastry

Combine the first 10 ingredients and, using hands, mix well. Let stand for 30 minutes, frequently tossing flavorings through the vegetables. Place ingredients in a strainer to allow excess liquid to drain away. Use 2 sheets of filo pastry per roll. Fold in half. Turn the filo pastry sheet around so that a corner faces you. Spread ingredients across the pastry. Turn corner over filling and wipe all remaining edges with water and cornstarch. Fold over edges and roll up into a long roll. Repeat with remaining ingredients.

Place on a non-stick baking sheet. Wipe over tops with soy sauce and water. Do not soak the pastry. Cook at 450°F for 20 minutes. Serve immediately.

Note: If wholemeal filo pastry is unavailable, use plain filo pastry and sprinkle wheat bran or oat bran between the sheets.

CHINESE WHOLE FISH

Serves 4–6

1 whole fish (3¹/₂ pounds)
1/4 cup lemon juice
4–6 cups chicken stock (see page 31)
1 mild onion, diced
1 stalk celery, diced
1 carrot in strips
1/2 inch piece ginger, finely chopped
2 cloves garlic, crushed
fresh coriander sprigs

Garnish

1 carrot, peeled and cut into
    julienne strips
2–3 green onions, finely sliced
    diagonally
1/2 cup wine vinegar
1/4 cup unsweetened orange juice
Combine and soak for 1 hour

Clean and scale fish. Rub the fish inside and out with lemon juice. Place the stock in a wok or large deep frying pan. Add vegetables, ginger and garlic. Bring to a boil over a low heat. Steam fish in the wok raising it in either a steamer or on a plate placed on top of an upturned bowl. After the fish has cooked, remove it. Boil the remaining stock quickly and spoon it over the fish. (Alternatively, place the fish in foil in a moderate oven for 30 minutes. Pour over 1 cup of stock and flavorings.)

Place fish on heated serving dish. Bring the remaining stock to a rapid boil until reduced slightly. Spoon over fish.

Drain the carrots, green onions and sprinkle over fish to garnish. Serve immediately. This dish may also be served cold. After cooking, cool, then refrigerate. Serve well chilled.

CURRIED SCALLOPS

Serves 12

36–40 scallops

Curry Sauce
1 clove garlic, crushed
1 medium onion, finely chopped
1/2 cup celery, finely chopped
1 tablespoon wholemeal plain flour
1–1 1/2 tablespoons curry powder
2 1/2 cups chicken stock (see page 31)
3 tablespoons tomato paste, salt free
1/2 cup cooked apple purée
1 tablespoon lemon juice
2 tablespoons finely chopped parsley
1/2–1 cup non-fat yogurt (optional)

Sauté garlic and onion in tablespoon of water until soft. Add celery, stir in wholemeal flour and curry powder and cook for 3 minutes, stirring continuously. Add chicken stock, tomato paste, apple purée and lemon juice. Cover and simmer for 30 minutes, stirring frequently. Add parsley.

May be stored in the refrigerator for use when required. It will keep for 1 week.

If a milder curry is required, add non-fat yogurt just prior to serving.

Cover scallops with boiling water. Bring to a gentle simmer. Turn off heat. Drain well. Add scallops to the curry sauce and fold through.

FISH IN MANGO SAUCE

Serves 4

8 fillets of firm white fish (2 ounces each)
chicken stock (see page 31)
lemon juice
black pepper

Sauce
1 cup dry white wine
1/2 cup non-fat yogurt
1 mango
black pepper to taste

Poach fillets in chicken stock. Season each fillet with black pepper to taste and a squeeze of lemon juice as it poaches. Poach for no more than 3 minutes either side. Remove carefully to a heated platter and keep warm.

To make the sauce, use the same pan as the fish has been poached in. Pour out any leftover stock. Pour in the white wine and yogurt and keep heat on high for liquid to reduce. Add the peeled and sliced mango as the sauce reduces. The mango only takes a couple of minutes to cook, so stir occasionally to move it from the bottom of the pan. The sauce takes approximately 4 minutes to cook and will turn a golden brown color. Place the fish fillets on serving plates and spoon a small amount of sauce over them.

SALMON BAKE

Serves 6–8

Base

1 cup cooked brown rice
3/4 pound broccoli, cooked and
* puréed*

Filling

12 ounce can salmon, salt free
* packed in water*
1 medium sized onion, finely
* chopped*
2 cups soy milk
1/4 cup cornstarch
1 teaspoon hot, low salt mustard
1 medium sized red bell pepper
1 medium sized green bell pepper

Combine rice and broccoli and mix well. Spoon onto a shallow lightly greased ovenproof dish.

Cook onion for 3 minutes in 2 tablespoons water. Add soy milk, keeping 1/4 cup aside. Blend this with the cornstarch to make a paste. Add to heated soy milk, stirring until it thickens. Cook gently for 2 minutes, stirring continuously. Add salmon and mustard and mix well. Remove from heat.

Chop peppers finely and cook in a small amount of water for 2 minutes to soften. Drain. Add to salmon. Pour over the base.

TUNA AND VEGETABLE PIE

Serves 6

Pie crust

6 slices wholemeal bread

Filling

1 medium sized onion, finely diced
1 1/2 cups low fat evaporated skim
* milk or soy milk*
1 tablespoon salt free tomato paste
1 cup tuna, water packed, salt free
1 cup carrot, grated
1 cup celery, finely diced
1 small green bell pepper, finely
* diced*
1/4 cup fresh parsley, finely chopped
2 tablespoons fresh chives, finely
* chopped*
4 tablespoons cornstarch
1/2 cup water

Crumble the bread into fine breadcrumbs. Lightly grease a small pie dish. Reserve 3/4 cup bread-crumbs for topping. Place breadcrumbs in pie dish and spread over base and sides evenly. Firm down with fingers and palm of your hand. Cook at 400°F for 10 minutes. Remove from oven. Turn oven up to 450°F.

While pie crust is cooling, cook onion in 1 tablespoon water for 3 minutes or until transparent. Add milk and simmer 2 minutes. Stir in tomato paste. Add tuna, carrot, celery and pepper. Simmer, covered, for 5 minutes. Add parsley and chives.

Mix the cornstarch with the water to make a thin paste. Stir this through the tuna mixture and cook for 2 minutes stirring continuously. Cool slightly. Pour into pie crust. Sprinkle with remaining bread-crumbs. Cook at 450°F for 10 minutes. Turn oven down to 400°F and cook for further 20 minutes. Serve with a tossed salad or lightly steamed vegetables.

SALMON MOUSSE

Serves 8

12 ounces red salmon (lightly cooked, salt free)
¼ cup lemon juice
¼ cup boiling water
1 tablespoon dijon mustard
¼ cup finely chopped celery
¼ cup cider vinegar
1 tablespoon gelatin
1 cup non-fat yogurt
¼ cup finely chopped green bell pepper
1 tablespoon finely grated fresh horseradish (optional)

Combine salmon, vinegar and lemon juice in a food processor and lightly purée. Dissolve gelatin in water. Add yogurt and mustard to salmon and purée to combine. Add gelatin and mix well. Fold through the remaining ingredients and pour into a glass mold. Refrigerate until quite firm. Serve with salad.

TUNA POTATO ROULADE

Serves 6–8

2¼ pounds peeled potatoes
¼ cup chopped green onions (green part only)
3 cups wholemeal breadcrumbs
1 egg white

Filling

6 ounces tuna (water packed)
1 cup chopped green onions (green part only)
1 apple, peeled and cut in quarters
10 medium mushrooms, washed
1 tablespoon lemon juice

Steam potatoes lightly until tender; drain and mash. Fold in ¼ cup green onions, breadcrumbs and egg white and mix well. Place a sheet of foil on a baking tray (approximately 12" x 14"). Lightly grease and sprinkle over wholemeal plain flour. While potato is still warm, spoon it in 'blobs' over the baking tray. Flatten down with the palm of your hand until flat (approximately ¼" thick).

Combine filling mixture in a food processor and using the stop start button lightly process. Spoon filling mixture along one edge of the longest side of foil. Press down firmly. Pick up the end of the foil at the same edge and begin to roll over. (If filling starts to fall, just keep pressing it back into position with your hand.) Keep rolling until there is no more potato. Use a knife or spatula to flatten edge onto the main roll to make an even finish.

Place carefully on a lightly greased baking tray. Cook in a hot oven 500°F for 30 minutes, turn heat down and cook for a further 30 minutes at 400°F.

Serve with lightly steamed julienne of vegetables in season. For example, carrot, celery, zucchini, yellow squash, cucumber, green onions.

TUNA BAKE

Serves 6

1 large can tuna in water, drained
3 cups cooked wholemeal macaroni
* or natural brown rice*
1 small can drained unsweetened
* pineapple pieces (optional)*
1 cup cooked corn kernels
1 cup chopped red and green bell
* peppers*
2 shallots, chopped
black pepper to taste
2 cups white sauce (see page 133)
1 cup wholemeal breadcrumbs
1/4 cup low fat cheese

Combine tuna, macaroni or rice, pineapple, corn, pepper, shallots and black pepper. Pour over white sauce, sprinkle top with breadcrumbs and cheese. Bake in a hot oven until top is golden brown and tuna is heated through. Serve with a tossed salad.

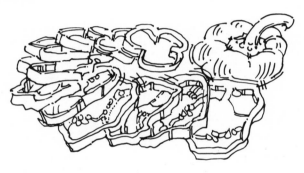

FISH PARCELS

Serves 4

4 fillets firm white fish (3 ounces)
4 tablespoons finely grated low fat
* grating cheese*
8 medium mushrooms, thinly sliced
1/4 cup non-fat yogurt
1 tablespoon finely chopped chives
2 tablespoons finely chopped red
* pepper*
cayenne pepper to taste
16 julienne strips of carrot
1 tablespoon non-fat yogurt (extra)
1 egg white
1/4 cup wholemeal breadcrumbs,
* toasted*

Spread fillets out flat to make a rectangle (pound slightly, if necessary). Combine cheese, mushrooms, yogurt, chives, pepper and cayenne. Mix well. Spread evenly over each fillet. Place 4 carrot strips on each fillet and carefully roll up. Place seam side down in a lightly greased shallow baking dish. Combine yogurt and egg white. Using a pastry brush, wipe the tops of fish and sprinkle over the breadcrumbs.

Bake at 350°F for 20 minutes. Serve with a salad.

WHITE FISH WITH LEMON SAUCE

Serves 6

1 pound fish fillets
2 cups cooked mashed potato
2 apples, peeled and grated
1 egg white
¹/₂ cup finely chopped green onions
  (white part only)
1 tablespoon finely chopped basil
  (fresh)
2 tablespoons finely chopped
  oregano (fresh)
¹/₄ cup non-fat yogurt

Lemon Sauce
¹/₂ cup lemon juice
¹/₂ cup unsweetened orange juice
1 tablespoon apple juice concentrate
2 tablespoons arrowroot

Brown Parsley Rice
3 cups cooked brown rice (hot)
1 cup chopped parsley

Tomato, Onion and Cucumber in
  Herb Vinaigrette
24 cherry tomatoes
2 onions, peeled and cut into thin
  wedges
1 cucumber, cut in half, seeds
  removed and sliced thinly to make
  a half-moon shape
1 cup herb vinaigrette (see page 57)

To cook fish Chop fish fillets into small pieces. Combine with all other ingredients. Lightly grease a mold (preferably a fish shape mold). Spoon mixture into mold and pack down firmly. Place in a water bath and cover with foil. Cook at 350°F for 30 minutes.

To make vegetable salad Combine all ingredients and pour over 1 cup of herb vinaigrette.

Lemon sauce Combine all ingredients. Stir over heat until sauce boils and thickens. Serve over the fish.

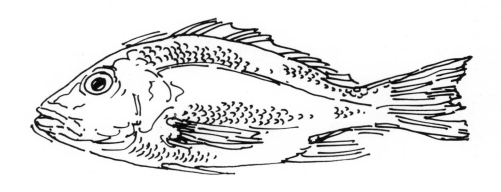

FISH VEGETABLE BUNDLES

Serves 6

6 fish fillets
julienne strips of carrot, zucchini,
  green beans, cucumber, red and
  green peppers (approximately
  9 – 10 strips per fillet)
1 cup non-fat yogurt
1/2 cup non-fat grating cheese, grated
1 cup wholemeal breadcrumbs
2 tablespoons fresh parsley, finely
  chopped
2 tablespoons fresh chives, finely
  chopped

Roll fish fillets to flatten slightly. Place combination of julienne vegetables in center of fillet with ends of vegetable visible at either side. Roll up. Place in a shallow, lightly greased ovenproof dish with seam side down. Pour over yogurt and sprinkle with cheese.

Combine breadcrumbs, parsley and chives. Sprinkle over fish. Cover with foil. Cook at 350°F for 20–30 minutes or until fish is tender. Remove foil for the last few minutes to brown and crisp breadcrumbs. Serve with salad or steamed vegetables and small steamed potatoes.

POULTRY

CHICKEN AND CARROT LOAF

Serves 6–8

1–1¹/₂ cups minced raw chicken
1 cup chopped parsley
2¹/₄ cups grated carrot (3–4 carrots)
1 small onion, chopped
¹/₂ cup fine wholemeal breadcrumbs
black pepper to taste
1¹/₄ cups natural non-fat yogurt with
 an added squeeze lemon juice

Combine chicken, ¹/₂ cup of parsley, 1¹/₂ cups carrot, onion, breadcrumbs, pepper and yogurt in a large bowl and mix well. Press ¹/₃ of the mixture into a glass terrine dish. Sprinkle the remaining carrots over the top and press down firmly. Add another ¹/₃ of the chicken mixture pressing down well, and sprinkle over remaining parsley. Top with chicken mixture and press firmly down. Cover with foil and bake in a water dish for 1 hour or until golden brown. Leave to cool in terrine. Gently ease a metal spatula around the sides of the chicken loaf, turn onto a plate and chill well before serving. Serve with salad and fresh wholemeal rolls. An excellent loaf for a picnic.

CHICKEN AND FRUIT CURRY

Serves 4–6

12 ounces chicken meat with skin
 and fat removed
2 cloves garlic, crushed
1 large onion, diced
1 tablespoon curry powder
2 cups chicken stock (see page 31)
2 bay leaves
12 ounces can unsweetened apricot
 halves, drained
12 ounces can unsweetened
 pineapple pieces, drained
6 water chestnuts, thinly sliced
1 cup soy milk or skim milk
1 tablespoon and 1 teaspoon
 cornstarch

Stir fry chicken on a hot non-stick surface to seal meat and lightly brown. This will take approximately 3 minutes. Remove chicken from pan. Add garlic, onion and curry powder. Toss continuously until onion is transparent (approximately 2–3 minutes).

Add chicken stock and bay leaves and bring to a boil. Add chicken meat and simmer for 20 minutes or until chicken is tender. Add apricots, pineapple and water chestnuts. Combine soy milk and corn-starch to make a paste. Add, stirring continuously until sauce boils and thickens. Serve with brown rice.

Note: When not using oil to brown, reduce cooking temperature so that food does not burn. Toss continuously.

CHICKEN AND GINGER ZUCCHINI BALLS

Serves 4–6
Makes 16–20

12 ounces chicken meat (all visible
  fat and skin removed)
2 green apples, peeled and grated
1 medium onion, peeled and chopped
2 medium zucchini, grated
1 teaspoon finely grated fresh ginger
1 teaspoon finely grated lemon rind
1 cup wholemeal breadcrumbs

Combine chicken, apples and onion in a food processor. Process until smooth. Remove from food processor bowl and add zucchini, ginger and lemon. Mix well. Take a spoonful of mixture and roll into a ball. Roll in breadcrumbs.

Place on a lightly greased oven tray and cook at 400°F for 30–40 minutes or until lightly browned.

Serve with a selection of salads.

CHICKEN OR VEAL PARCELS

1 piece of chicken breast or veal
  steak (approximately 4 ounces per
  person)

Marinade
dry white wine
unsweetened orange juice
lemon and lime juice
dry sherry and apple juice

Herbs
tarragon
sage
rosemary
garlic
marjoram
coriander
chervil
basil
dill

Marinate the chicken or veal for an hour, tossing frequently. Remove meat from marinade. Place onto a sheet of foil and add one or two of the suggested herbs. Add one of the following. Secure the parcel tightly and bake in a moderate oven for 30 minutes or until meat is tender.

Extras
fresh halved apricots
pitted red cherries
pineapple and pepper chunks
almonds
fresh peaches
chopped tomatoes and onion rings

Opposite:
Tuna potato roulade (p63)
Overleaf:
Fish parcels (p64) served with green beans

CHICKEN CHASSEUR

Serves 6–8

*2 pounds chicken drumsticks and
    wings with skin and fat removed*
1 pound carrot cut into chunks
14 ounces mushrooms
2 cloves garlic, crushed
2 tablespoons low salt soy sauce
1 cup dry white wine
*12 ounce can salt free tomatoes,
    puréed*
2 tablespoons salt free tomato paste
1/4 teaspoon dried tarragon
1/4 cup green onions, chopped
*2 tablespoons fresh parsley, finely
    chopped*

Sauce
1 onion, thinly sliced
1/2 cup grated parsnip
1/3 cup cornstarch
3 cups chicken stock (see page 31)

Stir fry chicken to seal meat and slightly brown. Remove chicken and set aside. Stir fry onion and parsnip until onion is transparent (approximately 3 minutes). Add combined cornstarch and stock. Bring to a boil, reduce heat and simmer for 10 minutes. Remove sauce from pan and set aside.

Wash pan and stir fry garlic and mushrooms in soy sauce until mushrooms are soft. Add wine and boil until liquid has reduced by half. Add combined puréed tomatoes, tomato paste and tarragon. Stir to combine.

Add onion and parsnip sauce to the pan. Add chicken and carrots. Cover or place all ingredients in a covered casserole dish. Cook at 400°F for 40 minutes or until chicken and carrots are tender. If cooking on top of the stove, keep casserole simmering, stirring occasionally so ingredients do not stick to the base of pan. Serve with brown rice, mashed potato or wholemeal noodles.

CHICKEN MACARONI

Serves 6

3 cups cooked wholemeal macaroni
2 cups chopped cooked chicken
1 can tomatoes, chopped and juice
1 cup celery, chopped
1 cup green bell pepper, chopped
1 cup grated carrot
1/4 cup chopped chives
1/4 cup chopped parsley
*1 teaspoon fresh ginger, grated
    (optional)*
black pepper to taste
*1 cup chicken or vegetable stock (see
    page 33)*

Combine all ingredients in an oven proof dish. Cover and cook in a moderate oven for 30–40 minutes or until well heated through.

Opposite:
Chicken chasseur (p69)
Previous page:
Beef burger with the lot (p73)
Chicken burger (p70)

CHICKEN BURGERS

Makes 4

*7 ounces chicken with fat and skin
removed*
1 green apple, peeled and grated
2 ounces low fat grating cheese
1 cup wholemeal breadcrumbs
*2 tablespoons fresh chives, finely
chopped*
*2 tablespoons fresh parsley, finely
chopped*

If doubling recipe, do not double quantity of cheese.
Add 1 ounce extra cheese for 7 ounces extra chicken.

Mince chicken. Add other ingredients and mix well.
Form into 4 balls and flatten. Cook in a non-stick pan
for 2 minutes on both sides. Serve in a wholemeal
burger bun or between 2 wholemeal pita breads. Add
shredded lettuce, cucumber slices, grated carrot,
alfalfa sprouts, thin slices of apple, bean sprouts or
sliced celery. Top with some home-made mango
chutney.

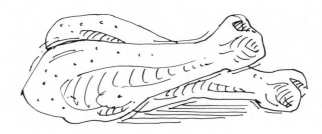

CHICKEN SWEET AND SOUR

Serves 6

*1 pound chicken with fat and skin
removed*
1 medium sized red bell pepper
1 medium sized green bell pepper
2 medium sized carrots
2 medium sized zucchinis
6 green onions
3 stalks celery
1/2 cup chopped pineapple

Sauce

1 cup unsweetened apple juice
*1 teaspoon fresh ginger, finely
chopped*
2 teaspoons low salt soy sauce
1 tablespoon salt free tomato paste
1 clove garlic, crushed (optional)

Cut chicken into 1 inch chunks. Cut vegetables into
even sized pieces. Combine all sauce ingredients in a
wok or large shallow pan. Bring to boil and simmer
gently. Add chicken. Cook for 15–20 minutes or until
tender.

Remove chicken. Turn up heat. Add all vegetables
and cook for 2 minutes, tossing continuously through
the sauce. Add chicken and pineapple. Place lid on
wok or pan and cook a further minute. Serve on a
bed of hot brown rice.

BREAST OF TURKEY WITH ORANGE CURRY SAUCE

Serves 10–12

2 pounds turkey breast (remove skin and visible fat)
1 onion
2 green apples
2 teaspoons finely grated orange rind
1 teaspoon dried sage
1 teaspoon dried thyme
1 cup dry white wine/water

Lightly pound the turkey breast. Peel and slice the onion and the apples. Place onion and apple slices on the bottom of a shallow baking pan. Place the turkey breast on top of the onion and apple. Sprinkle over orange rind, sage, thyme, and pour over white wine or water. Cover. Cook at 350°F for 2 hours. Meat is cooked when you insert a fine skewer through meat and juices are clear.

Let turkey stand for a few minutes before slicing. Use an electric knife to cut into 10 to 12 portions. Keep hot. Serve with orange curry sauce (see page 56).

ROAST TURKEY BREAST

Serves 10

2¼ pounds breast of turkey (fat removed)
1 clove garlic, crushed
2 tablespoons finely chopped onion
1½ tablespoons orange juice (unsweetened)
1 cup wholemeal breadcrumbs
6 medium mushrooms, sliced thinly
2 green onions, finely chopped
¼ teaspoon sage
½ teaspoon marjoram
2 medium carrots (cut into very thin circles)
1½ cups water

Gravy
1 tablespoon tomato paste
2 tablespoons cornstarch

Crunchy Baked Mushrooms
20 medium mushrooms
20 tablespoons non-fat cottage cheese
½ cup wholemeal breadcrumbs

Roast Cook the garlic and onion in the orange juice for 3 minutes until onion is soft. Add to the breadcrumbs, mushrooms, green onions and spices. Mix well.

Cut a pocket in the turkey breast. Fill the pocket with the mushroom, breadcrumb mixture. Secure with skewers.

In a baking dish, line the base with the carrot. Add the water. Lie the turkey breast on top. Cover with foil. Baste turkey every 15 minutes. Cook at 350°F for 1 hour.

Serve with dry baked potato, steamed carrots, peas and crunchy baked mushrooms.

Gravy Remove turkey from baking dish. Place juices and carrot in a blender. Add tomato paste. Blend until smooth. Pour into a pan and slowly bring to the boil. Make a·paste with the cornstarch and a small amount of water. Stir into the gravy to thicken. Spoon over the turkey slices.

Crunchy Baked Mushrooms Allow 2 mushrooms per person. Peel and remove stems. Top with a spoonful of cottage cheese and sprinkle over generously with wholemeal breadcrumbs. Cook at 400°F for 10 minutes or until well browned.

STEAMED WHOLE CHICKEN

Serves 4–6

1 chicken
1/2 lemon
1/4 cup unsweetened orange juice
   or 1/4 cup apple juice or 1/4 cup dry
   wine
1 1/2 cups water
sprigs of parsley
stick of celery with leaves
1/2 carrot
black pepper

Completely remove all skin and any visible fat pockets from chicken.

Place chicken in a pan just big enough to hold it and the vegetables. Place lemon in chicken cavity and pour over liquid. Place parsley, celery and carrot in pan around chicken and season with black pepper. Bring to a boil. Turn heat down to its lowest and simmer for 30 minutes with the lid on. Test to see if chicken is cooked and remove from stock. Wrap up securely in foil and leave to cool.

Variation
Garlic Chicken   Wipe the inside of the chicken with 2 cloves of crushed garlic. Follow instructions above but leave out the last four ingredients.

BEEF

BEEF AND CARROT HOTPOT

Serves 5

*1 pound beef with visible fat
  removed*
1 pound carrots, cut into chunks
2 cloves garlic
1 large onion
1 cup dry red wine
1/2–1 teaspoon nutmeg
2 cups beef stock or water
2 tablespoons salt free tomato paste
3 bay leaves
*2 tablespoons fresh parsley, finely
  chopped*

Cut meat into small pieces and then stir fry to seal and lightly brown. Remove from pan. Stir fry onions and garlic until onions are transparent (approximately 2–3 minutes). Return meat to pan. Add red wine and nutmeg and cook for 5 minutes. Add tomato paste and stock. Pour into a casserole dish. Add carrots and bay leaves. Toss well and cook at 400°F for 13/4 hours or until meat is tender. Add parsley before serving. Serve with hot mashed potato, brown rice or wholemeal noodles.

BEEF BURGER WITH THE LOT

Makes approximately 10 burgers

1 pound fat free minced beef
6 ounces carrot, grated
6 ounces zucchini, grated
6 ounces green apples, grated
12 ounces potato, peeled and grated
*1 cup wholemeal breadcrumbs,
  firmly packed*
2 tablespoons wholemeal plain flour
1/4 cup fresh parsley, finely chopped
1/2 teaspoon nutmeg
1/2 teaspoon dried mixed herbs

Combine all ingredients and mix with hands. Shape into equal size balls. Flatten down. Place in a lightly greased pan and cook on moderate heat for approximately 6 minutes. Carefully turn over and cook for a further 4–5 minutes. Remove from pan and rest on paper towels for a few minutes. Divide a wholemeal burger bun or use 2 wholemeal pita breads. Add shredded lettuce, onion rings, tomato slices, grated carrot, red and green bell pepper rings, bean sprouts.

BEEF AND BELL PEPPER

Serves 6

1 pound beef with visible fat
    removed
1 large onion, cut into 8 pieces
1 green bell pepper, cut into chunks
1 red bell pepper, cut into chunks
2 stalks celery, sliced diagonally

Sauce

1 teaspoon fresh ginger, finely
    chopped
1 tablespoon salt free tomato paste
1 tablespoon low salt soy sauce
1/2 teaspoon dried basil
1/2 teaspoon dried oregano
2 cups beef stock or water
2 tablespoons cornstarch

Slice meat into very thin strips. Stir fry meat (in 3 lots) to seal meat and lightly brown. Remove meat from pan. Add onion, peppers and celery and toss, cooking for 2 minutes. Return meat to pan.

Pour over combined sauce ingredients. Bring to the boil and then reduce heat. Simmer with lid on for 20–30 minutes. Stir occasionally so meat does not stick to base of pan. Serve with hot mashed potato or brown rice.

FRUITY BEEF LUNCHEON LOAF

Serves 10–12

5 ounces minced beef with visible fat
    removed
1 medium sized onion, finely diced
12 ounces potato, grated
12 ounces carrots, grated
4 ounces dried apricots, finely
    chopped
4 ounces golden raisins
4 ounces raisins
2 cups wholemeal breadcrumbs
1/3 cup salt free tomato paste
1 tablespoon low salt soy sauce
1/2–1 teaspoon cumin
1/2 teaspoon coriander powder
1/2 teaspoon mixed spice
5 cups wholemeal breadcrumbs (for
    topping)

Line a dish measuring approximately 16 inches x 12 inches x 2 inches with lightly greased foil. Press 2 cups breadcrumbs firmly onto base of dish. Combine all ingredients and mix well with hands. Pour into dish on top of breadcrumb base and press down. Top with breadcrumbs and press down again. Cook at 450°F for 20 minutes. Turn heat down to 375°F and cook for further 50–55 minutes. Remove from oven. If serving hot, let stand for 10 minutes before slicing.

This loaf is excellent served hot or cold with a salad.

CABBAGE ROLLS WITH TOMATO SAUCE

Makes 12

1/2 teaspoon cumin
1/4 teaspoon coriander
6 ounces carrot, grated
3 ounces zucchini, grated
2 cups cooked brown rice
18 large cabbage leaves (Choose
green cabbage with thin, soft
leaves, not a hard center white
cabbage, as the leaves break too
easily and tend to be stringy in
texture.)
1 pound ground round steak with
no visible fat
1 onion (approximately 3 oz)
1/2 teaspoon fresh ginger root
2 tablespoons water

Tomato sauce

12 ounces can salt free tomatoes in
juice
1/4 cup salt free tomato paste
1/4 cup water or dry white wine or
vegetable stock (see page 33)
1 large clove garlic
1/2 teaspoon cumin
fresh parsley, finely chopped to
garnish

White cheese sauce

1 cup soy milk
4 tbsps cornstarch
1/2 cup low fat grating cheese
ground black pepper to taste or a
pinch of cayenne pepper

Cook onion with ginger and spices in water until soft. Add ground round steak and separate it. Cover and simmer for 15–20 minutes. Continue to separate meat as it cooks, making sure all meat is well browned and cooked through. Remove from heat. Add all other ingredients and mix well. Cool.

Place cabbage leaves in boiling water and cook for 5 minutes to soften. Drain. Do 5 leaves at a time or use a large pan. Cut away the hard center core, but do not cut right through the leaf. Use 1 1/2 leaves to make a whole flat leaf. Use approximately half a cup of mixture to make each cabbage roll. Roll up securely, making sure the filling cannot ooze out from the sides.

Tomato sauce

Purée all ingredients. Pour half the sauce into the bottom of a large, shallow baking dish. Place cabbage rolls, seam side down, on top of sauce and pack tightly together. Pour over remaining sauce. Cover with foil. Cook at 400°F for 30 minutes. Remove foil and cook a further 15 minutes.

Serve with a boiled or baked potato and an orange vegetable (pumpkin, carrot) or with a tossed salad. Garnish with fresh parsley.

Alternative cooking methods Cabbage rolls can be steamed in a steamer for approximately 30–40 minutes. Tomato sauce can be cooked in a pan for 20 minutes or until thickened and poured over steamed cabbage rolls.

Variations Make other sauces, i.e. white cheese sauce to serve over steamed cabbage rolls.

White cheese sauce

Bring all but 1/4 cup soy milk to just below boiling. Make a paste with the remaining milk and cornstarch. Stir until it thickens. Cook for 2 minutes. Add cheese and stir until it melts. Season with pepper.
Or
Sprinkle a cup of wholemeal breadcrumbs over the top of cabbage rolls after 30 minutes cooking time. Cook for a further 15 minutes.
Or
Sprinkle over 1/2 cup low fat grating cheese 10 minutes before cabbage rolls are cooked. Cheese should be just melted, not well browned.

BEEF STROGANOFF

Serves 6

1 pound round steak with visible fat
  removed
2 medium sized onions
1/2 pound carrots, cut into thin
  rounds and then quartered
1 pound mushrooms, thinly sliced
1 tablespoon orange juice
1 cup boiling water
1 cup dry red wine
2 tablespoons salt free tomato paste
ground black pepper
1 cup soy milk or skim milk
1 tablespoon and 1 teaspoon
  cornstarch

Cut steak into bite size pieces. Stir fry to seal meat and lightly brown. Remove meat from the pan. Stir fry onions until transparent (approximately 2–3 minutes). Add carrots and mushrooms and toss to combine. Add orange juice to pan. Simmer for 3 minutes. Return meat to pan. Add red wine and tomato paste and season to taste with black pepper. Cook 1 1/4 hours at 400°F in a covered casserole dish. Combine soy milk and cornstarch. Remove casserole from heat and allow to cool slightly. Stir in the soy milk and cornstarch until sauce becomes thick and creamy. Serve with mashed or baked potatoes.

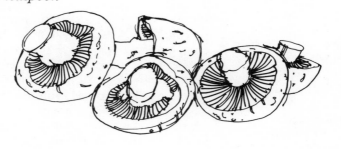

BAKED BUTTERNUT PUMPKIN

Serves 2

1 medium butternut pumpkin
1 clove garlic, crushed
2 tablespoons onion, finely chopped
2 tablespoons finely chopped red bell
  pepper
6 ounces minced beef (all visible fat
  removed)
1/2–1 teaspoon ground cumin
1 cup grated carrot
2 large chopped tomatoes, peeled
  and seeded
1 cup cooked brown rice
1 cup wholemeal breadcrumbs
2 tablespoons finely grated low fat
  grating cheese

Cut pumpkin in half lengthwise. Scoop out seeds and some of the pumpkin flesh to leave a deep cavity. Crush garlic, add onion, pepper and meat in a small pan. Add a small amount of water. Cook on low heat for 20 minutes or until meat is tender. Turn frequently. Add spices, grated carrot and tomatoes. Cover and cook over gentle heat for a further 5 minutes. Add more liquid if necessary (however, mixture should be fairly dry). Remove from heat and fold in rice.

Spoon equal quantities of mixture into the two pumpkin halves. Top with breadcrumbs and sprinkle over equal quantities of the cheese. Place in an oven bag or onto a baking tray, and cover with foil. Cook at 400°F for 40 to 45 minutes or until top is well browned.

SPAGHETTI AND MEATBALLS

Serves 8

Meat Balls
8 ounces fat free ground beef
1 onion, finely minced
1 mashed banana
1 apple, finely grated
black pepper to taste

Tomato Sauce
1 onion, diced
1/2 green bell pepper, finely diced
1 stalk celery, finely diced
12 ounces can tomatoes, chopped
2 tablespoons tomato paste
1 clove garlic, crushed
1/2 teaspoon basil
1/2 teaspoon oregano
black pepper to taste
chopped fresh parsley to garnish

Combine all ingredients and roll into very small balls. Place in a frypan in 11/2 inches of water which has been boiled and is just simmering. Cook for 8 minutes, turning once. Remove from pan and drain well. Keep hot.

Stir fry onion, green bell pepper and celery in 2 tablespoons water for 3 minutes. Add all other ingredients and simmer for 40 minutes.

Place hot spaghetti on serving plates, divide the meatballs evenly and pour over the tomato sauce.

ZUCCHINI MEATLOAF

Serves 10–12

14 ounces zucchini, grated
1 pound fat free ground round steak
*1 medium sized onion, finely
  chopped*
*3 ounces red bell pepper, finely
  chopped*
2 cups wholemeal breadcrumbs
1 egg white
2 tablespoons salt free tomato paste
*1 tablespoon fresh tarragon or
  parsley, finely chopped*
*1 tablespoon fresh basil, finely
  chopped*
*ground black pepper to taste
  (optional)*
1/4 cup low fat grating cheese, grated

Combine all ingredients except cheese. Using hands mix all ingredients thoroughly. Press mixture into a foil lined terrine dish. Press down firmly and cover with foil. Place terrine in a large pan of water so that the water reaches at least 1 inch up the side of the terrine dish. Cook at 350°F for 11/4 hours.

Drain off any liquid and unmold terrine onto a foil lined baking tray. Sprinkle over cheese. Return to oven and cook a further 10 minutes. Let stand 10 minutes before slicing if serving hot, or cool and refrigerate.

Serve as a meat luncheon loaf with salads or use in sandwiches or on wholemeal crackers.

VEGETARIAN ENTREES

CABBAGE CHOP SUEY

Serves 6–8

1 pound Chinese cabbage, shredded
4 ounces mushrooms, chopped
4 ounces beans, chopped
4 celery sticks, diagonally sliced
2 onions, cut into thin wedges
1 large carrot, diced
1 small red bell pepper, chopped
1 small green bell pepper, chopped
6 ounces fresh bean sprouts
1 teaspoon ginger root, finely
  chopped
1 clove garlic, crushed
2 tablespoons low salt soy sauce
1 tablespoon salt free tomato paste
2 tablespoons dry sherry or Chinese
  wine
1 1/2 cups Chinese chicken stock (see
  page 31)
1 tablespoon cornstarch

Optional extras
8 ounces lightly steamed chicken,
  cut into bite size pieces
or
8 ounces cooked shrimp, shelled and
  with back vein removed
or
1/2 cup almonds, roasted under grill
  until dark brown

Place ginger, garlic, soy sauce, tomato paste, sherry, 1/2 cup stock and mushrooms in a cold wok. Slowly bring to a boil and simmer, covered, for 1 minute.

Remove lid and add beans, celery and onions. Toss to combine all ingredients. Cook, covered, for 2 minutes.

Remove lid and add carrot, peppers and cabbage. Toss to combine all ingredients. You will need to do this at least twice as the cabbage softens. Cook, covered, for 3 minutes.

Remove lid and add the remaining stock combined with the cornstarch. Stir until sauce boils and begins to thicken. Add bean sprouts and optional extras. Toss ingredients to combine and cook for a further 2–3 minutes. Serve immediately.

CHILLI VEGETARIAN

Serves 10–12

2 cups red kidney beans
2 small onions
2 cloves garlic, crushed
8 ounces carrots
12 ounces green beans
2 small red bell peppers
1 cup salt free tomato juice
2 x 12 ounce cans salt free tomatoes
  and juice
1–2 teaspoons chilli powder or
  chopped fresh chilli, as much as
  you like
1/2 cup fresh parsley, finely chopped

Cover beans with water and soak overnight. Drain. Cover with clean cold water. Bring to the boil, reduce heat and simmer for 1 hour or until beans are tender. Drain and reserve cooking liquid.

Cook onion and garlic in a little water until soft and transparent (approximately 3 minutes). Add vegetables and 1/2 cup of cooking liquid from the beans. Simmer until vegetables begin to soften. Add tomato juice, tomatoes and chilli powder. Cook gently for 20 minutes. Add beans. Sprinkle over parsley and serve. Serve in a scooped out baked potato. Mash extra potato for topping. Reheat.
or
Fill a large scooped out tomato with chilli con carne beans. Cook in a moderately hot oven for 10 minutes or until tomato is soft.

MUSHROOM PIE

Serves 6–8

Base
2 cups wholemeal breadcrumbs
1/2 cup finely chopped shallots
1 egg white
1 tablespoon toasted sesame seeds

Filling
3 medium grated zucchini
2 medium sliced tomatoes
1 teaspoon basil, dried
1 teaspoon oregano, dried
6 ounces mushrooms, thinly sliced
4 egg whites
1/2 cup low fat evaporated milk
1 cup parsley, finely chopped
1/4 cup non-fat yogurt
1/4 cup low fat grating cheese
1 cup wholemeal breadcrumbs

To make base   Combine base ingredients in a food processor. Process until breadcrumbs begin to stick together. Do not overprocess. Lightly grease a fluted pie dish and press crumbs firmly over base and sides. Cook at 350°F for 15 minutes.

To make filling   Spread zucchini over base. Top with slices of tomato. Sprinkle over basil and oregano. Add mushrooms. Beat egg whites and milk. Add parsley and pour over mushrooms. Spoon yogurt in a circle over mushrooms. Sprinkle cheese over yogurt. Sprinkle over breadcrumbs. Cook at 400°F for 40 to 50 minutes.

FRESH TOMATO MOUSSE

Serves 4–6

2 pound ripe tomatoes
2 tablespoons gelatin
1/2 cup boiling water
1 egg white
1 cup non-fat yogurt
2 tablespoons tomato paste (salt and
  sugar free)
2 tablespoons finely chopped red bell
  pepper
2 tablespoons finely grated
  cucumber
2 tablespoons finely chopped fresh
  herbs (parsley, basil, oregano)

Peel the tomatoes. Cut in half and scoop out as many seeds as possible. Pour boiling water over gelatin and stir to dissolve. Leave to cool slightly. Place tomatoes and tomato paste in a blender and purée until smooth. Add gelatin and then the yogurt. Fold in the red bell pepper, grated cucumber and herbs. Beat egg white until stiff. Fold through mixture until just combined. Pour into individual molds and refrigerate until quite firm.

CHINESE CORN AND VEGETABLE COMBINATION

Serves 6

2 teaspoons fresh ginger root, finely
  chopped
2 cloves garlic, crushed
1 tablespoon low salt soy sauce
2 tablespoons Chinese wine or dry
  sherry
1/2 cup unsweetened orange juice
2 medium sized onions, cut into
  quarters
3 sticks celery, sliced diagonally
8 ounces green beans, sliced
  diagonally
8 ounces carrots sliced diagonally
4 ounces mushrooms sliced
4 ounces snow peas stringed, topped
  and tailed
6 ounce can baby corn, rinsed to
  remove salt
8 ounces fresh bean sprouts
1 cup Chinese chicken stock (see
  page 31)
1 tablespoon cornstarch

Add the first 5 ingredients to a cold wok. Slowly bring to a boil and simmer for 2 minutes.

Add onion and celery. Toss to combine ingredients and cook, covered, for 2 minutes

Add beans, carrot, mushrooms and snow peas. Toss and cook for 3 minutes.

Add corn and cook, covered, for 1 minute. Pour over combined stock and cornstarch and heat again to boiling. Add bean sprouts. Cook, covered, for 1 minute. Serve immediately.

PIZZA PARTY FOR 15–20

Makes approximately 30 slices

5 large pita breads,
or
2 pound pack wholemeal salt free
bread mix

Pizza sauce
Makes approximately 5 cups

3 medium sized onions, diced
2 cloves garlic, crushed
2 x 12 ounce cans salt free tomatoes,
puréed
1 cup salt free tomato paste
¹/₂ teaspoon basil
1 teaspoon oregano

Make up breadmix as instructed and add a teaspoon oregano to dry flour (optional). Let bread dough sit for 10–15 minutes. Divide into 5 pieces. Use a rolling pin to roll out to fit round pizza trays or place on large baking trays. Cover and stand for 15 minutes. Top with the following.

Cook onions and garlic in a little water until soft. Add remaining ingredients and boil for 5 minutes to thicken. Set aside to cool.

MUSHROOM PIZZA

Makes 1

1 cup pizza sauce
6 ounces mushrooms, finely chopped
3 ounces low fat grating cheese,
finely grated

Spread 1 cup pizza sauce over base. Sprinkle over mushrooms and cover with cheese. Cook for 10–15 minutes at 400°F.

HAWAIIAN PIZZA

Makes 2

2 cups pizza sauce
4 ounces green bell pepper, cut into
strips
4 ounces red bell pepper, cut into
strips
12 ounces unsweetened pineapple,
crushed and well drained
3 ounces low fat grating cheese,
finely grated

Divide ingredients equally between two bases. Spread 1 cup pizza sauce over each base. Add bell peppers, pineapple and top with cheese. Cook for 10–15 minutes at 400°F.

VEGETARIAN PIZZA

Makes 2

2 cups pizza sauce
6 ounces low fat grating cheese,
   finely grated
6 ounces carrots, cut into thin
   rounds and lightly cooked until
   just soft
6 ounces zucchini, cut into thin
   rounds and lightly cooked until
   just soft
4 ounces tomato, cut into thin
   round slices

Divide ingredients equally between 2 bases. Spread 1 cup pizza sauce over each base. Sprinkle cheese over pizza base. Place carrot and zucchini rounds over cheese. Top with slices of tomato. Cook for 10–15 minutes at 400°F. Serve with a large tossed salad.

PUMPKIN ALMOND PIE

Serves 8

Base
1 cup wheatgerm
1 cup wholemeal breadcrumbs

Filling
1 pound pumpkin, peeled and
   grated
4 potatoes, peeled and grated
2 cups wholemeal breadcrumbs
1 onion, peeled and grated
1 cup celery, finely chopped
1/4 teaspoon nutmeg
1/4 teaspoon cayenne pepper
4 egg whites
1/2 cup skim milk

Topping
1/2 cup bran
1/2 cup flaked almonds

Line a round 8 inch cake pan with foil. Combine wheat-germ and breadcrumbs. Press down well in the base of the cake pan.

Combine the filling ingredients and mix well. Press this mixture firmly onto the base.

Mix the bran and almonds and sprinkle over the filling. Cover with foil. Bake in a moderate oven for 1 1/2 hours. Remove foil and cook a further 10 minutes until almonds brown slightly. Serve hot or cold.

If you are serving the pie hot, let it stand for a few minutes and pull the foil up and pie can be removed easily and transferred to a serving plate.

PUMPKIN AND TOMATO QUICHE

Serves 6–8

Base
4 sheets wholemeal filo pastry

Filling
18 ounces cooked pumpkin
1 cup low fat evaporated skim milk
1 cup finely chopped shallots
1/2 cup finely chopped parsley
4 egg whites
black ground pepper to taste
  (optional)
1 teaspoon of curry powder
2 medium tomatoes

Lightly grease a 12 inch quiche flan. Place pastry sheets (one on top of the other) in flan. Neaten around edges. Place pumpkin and evaporated milk in a blender and process until smooth. Add shallots, parsley and stir through lightly beaten egg whites. Add pepper or curry powder. Pour over pastry. Slice tomatoes thinly and place over the top of pie.
  Cook at 350°F for 60 minutes or until firm.

Note: If wholemeal filo pastry is not available, use plain filo pastry and sprinkle wheat bran or oat bran between sheets.

RICE MOLD

Serves 8–10

3 cups brown rice
1 cup peas
1 cup grated carrot
1/2 cup green bell pepper, finely
  chopped
1/2 cup red bell pepper, finely
  chopped
1 cup alfalfa sprouts
1 cup green onions
1 cup celery
1/2 cup cucumber, peeled, seeded
  and chopped
1/2 cup fresh chopped herbs
2 tablespoons garlic vinaigrette (see
  page 56)
1/2 cup cooked puréed apple
1/4 teaspoon cayenne pepper

Cook rice in boiling water for 20 minutes. Add peas and cook for a further 5 minutes. Drain. Set aside to cool slightly. Combine all other ingredients and mix well while rice is still warm. Lightly grease a deep mold and firmly press rice mixture in. Press down firmly around the top. Cover with foil and refrigerate at least 4 hours prior to serving.
  Serve a slice on a bed of lettuce with chunks of fresh pineapple and cherry tomatoes.

Note: To get a good firm shape, place a weight on top of the firmed down rice while it is refrigerated.

Opposite:
Rice mold (p84)
Overleaf:
Beef and bell pepper (p74)
Beef and carrot hotpot (p73)
Beef stroganoff (p76)

SPINACH LASAGNE

Serves 6–8

*Take approximately 24 sheets
spinach lasagne noodles (made
from semolina and spinach)*

Vegetable Sauce
2 cloves garlic
1/2 cup thinly sliced celery
*1 cup green beans (top and tail, and
cut into small pieces)*
*1 cup zucchini (top and tail, cut
into thin rounds and then into 4)*
*1 cup carrot (wash, cut into thin
rounds and roughly chop into
small pieces)*
*1 cup red bell pepper (cut in half
and remove seeds, cut into strips
and roughly chop into small
pieces)*
1 teaspoon dried oregano
1 teaspoon dried rosemary
*12 ounce can salt and sugar free
tomatoes and juice*
8 ounces fresh spinach
2 small onions
1/2 cup thinly sliced mushrooms
1 teaspoon dried basil
1 1/2 cup water or dry white wine
*1/3 cup tomato paste (salt free and
sugar free)*
1/2 lemon

White Sauce
2 cups soy milk or skim milk
4 tablespoons cornstarch
2 bay leaves
3 ounces low fat grating cheese

Opposite:
Tuna and vegetable pie (p62) Zucchini moussaka (p88)
Salmon bake (p62)
Previous page:
Mushroom pie (p80)

Drop lasagne noodles one at a time into a large pan of boiling water. Add 1/2 cut lemon to the boiling water. When noodles are cooked remove and drop into chilled water. Leave here until required. Drain well before using.

Crush garlic and chop onions finely. Cook gently with a small amount of water, with the lid on for 3 minutes. Add all the vegetables and herbs and pour over the water or wine. Replace lid and cook for 10 minutes. Add tomatoes and juice. Leave lid off and let bubble for 20 minutes. Add tomato paste and cook for a further 10 minutes. Stir occasionally so that the vegetables do not stick to the bottom of the pan. Remove from heat.

Place spinach in a pan with boiling water and cook for 2 minutes. Drain well.

Place 1 3/4 cups soy milk and bay leaves in a pan. Slowly bring to a boil. Mix remaining soy milk with cornstarch to make a paste. Stir through the milk briskly before it comes to a boil. Stir all the time while sauce thickens (approximately 2 minutes). Place a layer of noodles in the bottom of a large lasagne dish. Pour over some vegetable sauce and top with a layer of noodles. Pour over half of remaining vegetable sauce, top with spinach and half the white sauce, and top with another layer of noodles. Pour over remaining sauce, top with noodles. Spread remaining white sauce evenly over the top layer of noodles and sprinkle with the grated cheese. Cook in a moderate oven for 30–40 minutes or until heated through and top is lightly browned. Stand 10 minutes before slicing into portions.

SPAGHETTI AND SPINACH SAUCE

Serves 6

1 quantity of wholemeal spaghetti

Sauce
2 bunches spinach
2 cloves garlic
2 ounces pinenuts
2 teaspoons chopped fresh basil or
  1/2 teaspoon dry basil
1/4 cup chopped parsley
black pepper to taste

Wash spinach and place leaves in water in a pan. Cover and bring to the boil. Reduce heat and simmer for 5 minutes. Put spinach in blender with crushed garlic, pinenuts, basil and parsley. Blend until smooth using a little of the cooking liquid if necessary. Season with black pepper.

Place spaghetti on serving plates and spoon over spinach sauce.

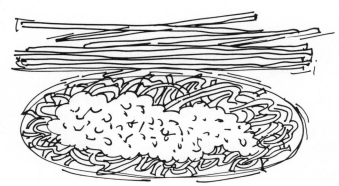

TOMATO CHEESE QUICHE

Serves 4–6

3 cups wholemeal breadcrumbs
2 tablespoons salt free tomato juice

Filling
1 medium sized onion, diced
12 ounce can salt free tomatoes
1/2 teaspoon basil
1/2 teaspoon oregano
1/2 teaspoon coriander powder
12 ounces low fat ricotta cheese
4 egg whites
2 large tomatoes
1 cup low fat grating cheese, finely
  grated

Combine base ingredients and press firmly into 9 inch round lightly greased pie dish. Bake at 350°F for 10–15 minutes or until lightly browned. Remove from oven and leave to cool.

Cook onion in a little water until soft (approximately 2–3 minutes). Remove from heat, add tomatoes, basil, oregano, coriander and ricotta cheese. Purée until very smooth. Beat egg whites until light and fluffy and gently fold into tomato mixture. Pour the mixture over the cooked breadcrumb base. Carefully lay slices of tomato on top to cover and spread cheese evenly over the tomato. Cook at 450°F for 15 minutes and turn down to 375°F for a further 30 minutes.

Garnish top with extra slices of tomato and fresh parsley. This quiche is delicious either hot or cold.

SPROUTS DAGWOOD

Serves 1–2

*2 slices salt free wholemeal or grain
  bread*
*2 tablespoons mango chutney (see
  page 136)*
*1/4–1/2 cup mung bean or lentil
  sprouts*
2 large slices tomato
4 slices cucumber with skin removed
1/4–1/2 cup alfalfa sprouts
cherry tomatoes

Spread one slice of bread with mango chutney. Spread mung bean or lentil sprouts evenly over the top. Add slices of tomato, cucumber and top with alfalfa sprouts and the second slice of bread.

Thread cherry tomatoes onto a long wooden skewer to the top end. Place skewer through the center of the sandwich to keep layers in place.

HOT CURRIED VEGETABLES

Serves 4

2 cups chicken stock (see page 31)
1 clove garlic, crushed
1 teaspoon turmeric
3/4 teaspoon chilli powder
*1/2 teaspoon ground ginger
  or 1 teaspoon grated fresh ginger*
1 teaspoon ground coriander

(If you do not like very hot curries, use only half the measurements given. If you are using fresh ginger you can still use a full teaspoon measure.)

Vegetables
*Equal quantity of
carrot strips
zucchini, cut into 1 inch lengths
celery, cut diagonally
green beans, cut into 1 inch pieces
cauliflower flowerettes
red and green bell pepper strips
mushrooms, peeled and sliced
12 ounce can whole tomatoes and
  juice
1/2 cup chopped shallots*

Bring stock and spices to a boil. Turn down heat. Add vegetables and simmer until vegetables are just tender. Add can of tomatoes and shallots and heat through. Serve with rice or noodles, a tossed green salad, chilled apple slices and a bowl of cucumber yogurt.

ZUCCHINI STUFFED WITH CHILLI BEANS

Serves 6

3 large zucchini
1 cup wholemeal breadcrumbs
1 cup low fat grating cheese

Chilli Beans

3 ounces Adsuki beans
12 ounce can salt free tomatoes
2 small red chillies (for a milder
    flavor use a medium sized red bell
    pepper)
2 green onions, finely chopped
1 clove garlic, crushed
1/4 teaspoon cumin
1/4 teaspoon dried oregano
2 tablespoons salt free tomato paste

Soak beans overnight. Drain and discard any beans that have not absorbed the water. Place in a clean pan and cover with water. Bring to a boil. Reduce heat, cover and simmer for 1–1 1/2 hours or until beans are tender. Drain. Chop tomatoes and add to pan with juice. Add very finely chopped chillies, green onions, garlic, spices and tomato paste. Cook for 15 minutes, stirring occasionally.

Cut zucchini in half lengthwise and scoop out seeds and some flesh. Chop flesh finely and add to tomato mixture. Cook a further 5 minutes. Add beans and keep hot.

Lightly steam zucchini until just tender. Fill zucchini with bean mixture. Place in a non-stick casserole. Sprinkle over breadcrumbs and the cheese. Cook in a hot oven for 15 minutes. Serve.

ZUCCHINI MOUSSAKA

Serves 6–8

1 pound large zucchini, cut into
    thin slices
1 onion, finely diced
2 cloves garlic, crushed
8 ounces carrots, finely diced
8 ounces mushrooms, finely diced
3 bay leaves
1 teaspoon oregano
1 teaspoon basil
2 x 12 ounces cans salt free
    tomatoes and juice
1/4 cup salt free tomato paste

White Sauce

2 cups soy milk or skim milk or
    evaporated skim milk
4 tablespoons cornstarch
dash of cayenne pepper
1 tablespoon skim milk herb cheese
1 cup grated low fat grating cheese

Cook zucchini until just tender and drain. Cook onion and garlic in 2 tablespoons water until soft and transparent. Add remaining ingredients except tomato paste and simmer, covered, for 15 minutes. Remove bay leaves and chop up tomatoes using a wooden spoon. Add tomato paste. Turn heat up and cook, uncovered, until sauce thickens, stirring occasionally.

Place soy milk in pan, reserving 1/4 cup. Blend 1/4 cup soy milk with cornstarch to make a paste. Bring milk to almost boiling and stir in cayenne pepper and skim milk herb cheese. Add cornstarch and stir continuously until sauce thickens.

Lightly grease an oblong ovenproof dish with high sides. Place a layer of zucchini on the base of the dish. Pour over a layer of sauce, enough to spread and cover zucchini. Repeat with alternate layers of zucchini and sauce. Top with layer of white sauce. Sprinkle over cheese. Cook at 375°F for 20–30 minutes or until cheese has melted and is brown and bubbling.

VEGETABLE SHEPHERD'S PIE

Serves 6

This is an adaptation of one of my favorite meals as a child. You can use any vegetable combination depending on what's in season or more importantly what's in your vegetable tray at the time.

Vegetables

2 medium carrots, peeled and cubed
1 potato, peeled and cubed
12 brussels sprouts, cut in half
1 medium zucchini, cut into slices
4 ounces cauliflower flowerettes
4 ounces broccoli flowerettes
3/4 cup green beans, cut into small
  pieces
3 ounces pumpkin, peeled and
  cubed
1/2 cup grated parsnip
3 ounces chopped cabbage

Gravy

1 onion, peeled and sliced
2 cloves garlic, crushed
2 cups vegetable/chicken stock (see
  page 31)
1 tablespoon tomato paste
2 tablespoons cornstarch
2 tablespoon water
1/4–1/2 cup chopped parsley

Topping

3–4 cups hot mashed potato
  (approximately 8 medium potatoes)

Place all vegetables in the top of a steamer and lightly steam for 12 minutes.

Sauté onion and garlic in 2 tablespoons of stock for 2 minutes. Add stock and stir in tomato paste. Combine cornstarch and water to make a paste. As the gravy begins to bubble, stir cornstarch paste into it. Add parsley. Cook for 5 minutes on a low heat, stirring continuously. Spoon vegetables into a suitable casserole or baking dish. Spoon over the gravy.

Spread the potato over the vegetables and gravy evenly by using a fork (this will give an interesting effect to the top of the pie, once it is cooked). Place in a water bath and cook at 450°F for 40 minutes.

RATATOUILLE

Serves 4

1/2 cup stock or water
2 white onions, cut into wedges (cut
   in half, in half again and repeat
   until wedges are small enough)
2 cloves garlic, crushed
2 egg plants, coarsely chopped
2 zucchini, sliced
4 tomatoes, peeled and chopped
2 bell peppers, chopped
6 green beans, chopped
1 stick celery, chopped
10 cauliflower flowerettes
1 carrot, thinly sliced
1 teaspoon dried basil and 1
   teaspoon celery seed

In a large frying pan add stock, onions and garlic. Cover and cook for 2 minutes over a gentle heat. Add egg plant and zucchini, cook for 5 minutes. Add tomatoes and all other ingredients. Sprinkle over herbs. Move around the pan for 10 minutes. Serve on a bed of brown rice or wholemeal toast.

VEGETABLES

'Does not nature produce enough simple vegetable foods to satisfy? And if not content with such simplicity can you not, by the mixture of them, produce infinite variations?'

— Leonardo Da Vinci

Vegetables offer a variety of shape, color and texture; they are a presentation delight for any cook, can be served as hors d'oeuvres, in a soup, as an accompaniment to the main meal or, in a combination, become the main meal itself.

However, of far greater importance is the fact that vegetables contain an abundance of vitamins and minerals. All vegetables should be prepared and cooked properly or they lose their flavor, their color and their valuable nutrients.

Do not soak vegetables in water before cooking as their goodness is readily absorbed by the water. Likewise, do not boil vegetables in water which is then discarded. Vegetables contain a lot of water, so there is no need to drown them in the cooking process. Vegetables should be lightly steamed so that they retain a slight crispness.

Unless the skins are hard or inedible most vegetables do not have to be peeled before cooking. A great deal of the desirable goodness is in the skins.

You can enhance the flavor of vegetables by adding fruit juices, herbs or a sauce.

Vegetables are an excellent food eaten raw and provide a wholesome between meal snack.

BEANS WITH GINGER AND GARLIC

8 ounces green beans
1 clove garlic, crushed
1 inch piece of ginger, sliced and
   finely chopped
squeeze of lemon juice
1/4 cup water

Toss beans with garlic and ginger and add a squeeze of lemon juice. Add water. Heat wok or large non-stick pan. Put vegetables in and, stirring constantly, cook for 3–4 minutes. Serve immediately.

STUFFED AND BAKED BEETS

Serves 4

4 medium size beets
grated apple
grated onion
chopped celery
chopped pepper
wholemeal breadcrumbs
squeeze of lemon juice
black pepper to taste

Peel beets. Cut the top away and make a hole in each beet using an apple corer. Mix all the ingredients and fill the beet. Wrap beets in foil and bake in a moderate oven in a water bath for 1 hour or until they are tender.

SWEET CINNAMON BEETS

Serves 4

8 baby beets
1 cup unsweetened orange juice
2 tablespoons grated orange rind
1–2 teaspoons cinnamon

Wash beets and place in a pan. Cover with orange juice and add rind and cinnamon. If there is not enough liquid, add 1/2 cup water. Gently simmer for 1 hour or until beets are tender. Add more water if necessary during the cooking. Peel and serve immediately.

LEMON MINT CARROTS

Serves 4–6

1 pound carrots, cut into sticks
1/2 cup chicken stock (see page 60)
1 tablespoon mint, chopped
juice of 1/2 lemon

Steam carrots lightly in chicken stock. Drain. Squeeze over lemon juice and sprinkle with mint. Let stand for 5 minutes before serving.

CARROT AND SUNFLOWER SEED BAKE

Serves 4

2¹/₂ cups carrot, sliced
1 small onion, finely chopped
¹/₂ cup water
black pepper to taste
1 tablespoon honey
¹/₄ cup soy grits (ground soya beans)
2 tablespoon dill, finely chopped
¹/₄ cup sunflower seeds
2 egg whites, lightly beaten
¹/₄ cup chopped almonds

Place carrots, onion and water in a pan and bring to a boil. Cover and simmer until carrots are just tender. Stir in all other ingredients except almonds. Pour into a shallow baking dish, sprinkle with almonds and bake for 15 minutes in a low oven.

CAULIFLOWER IN SESAME SAUCE

Serves 6–8

1 cauliflower, broken into pieces
1 quantity of white sauce (see page 133)
¹/₄ cup sesame seeds

Lightly steam cauliflower. Heat white sauce. Toast sesame seeds under grill. Place cauliflower pieces in a serving dish, cover with white sauce and sprinkle over sesame seeds. Place in a moderate oven for 10 minutes and serve.

CAULIFLOWER CHEESE BAKE

Serves 4

8 ounces carrots, cut into rounds
1 pound cauliflower, cut into flowerettes
2 cups soy milk
2 bay leaves
black pepper to taste
2 tablespoons parsley, finely chopped
4 tablespoons cornstarch
3 ounces low fat grating cheese, finely grated

Steam carrots and cauliflower until just tender. Combine remaining ingredients except cornstarch and cheese in a small pan. Combine cornstarch with a small amount of water to make a paste. Bring the soy milk and ingredients to just below boiling. Stir through the cornstarch briskly to make a thick sauce. Remove bay leaves.

Place carrots on the base of a shallow casserole. Top with cauliflower and pour over the white sauce. Sprinkle over with cheese. Cook at 400°F for 10–15 minutes or until top is browned.

93

CORN FRITTERS

Serves 6

2 cups corn
1 onion, finely chopped
3 egg whites
1/4 cup skim milk
1 cup plain wholemeal flour
1/2 teaspoon paprika

Combine all ingredients. Drop spoonfuls onto a non-stick pan and cook for 3 minutes and turn to brown the other side.

STUFFED ONIONS

Serves 6

6 large onions
wholemeal breadcrumbs
1 grated apple
1 cup finely chopped celery
1/4 cup finely chopped almonds
pinch allspice
1 egg white
juice of one small lemon
1/2 cup low fat finely grated cheese

Peel onions and cut in half crosswise. Carefully remove the centers. Chop the centers very finely and add to breadcrumbs, apple, celery, almonds and allspice. Fill onions with this mixture. Place onions in a pan with 2 1/2 inches of water to cover base of pan. Add the lemon juice. Cover and simmer for 45 minutes. Remove and sprinkle grated cheese over the top of each onion. Place under a hot broiler for a few minutes until golden brown.

PARSNIP FRITTERS

Serves 4

12 pieces parsnip, peeled and sliced
  into thin rings
black pepper or onion flakes to taste
wholemeal flour
1 egg white and skim milk
wholemeal breadcrumbs

Lightly steam parsnip rings until tender. Drain well and dry on kitchen paper. Sprinkle lightly with black pepper or onion flakes. Dip in flour, then in egg white and skim milk and coat with bread-crumbs. Gently fry in a non-stick pan until both sides are golden brown.

MINT PEAS

Serves 4

4 cups peas, shelled
1/2 cup chicken stock (see page 31)
several lettuce leaves
1 cup shallots, chopped
1/4 cup mint, chopped

Choose very young, tender peas. Shell peas. Allow 1 cup per person. In a shallow pan, pour 1/2 cup chicken stock. Place enough lettuce leaves on base of pan to hold peas so that they do not actually come in contact with the stock. Add 1 cup chopped shallots and 1/4 cup of chopped mint. Add peas, shallots and mint to the pan. Cover and cook over medium heat, shaking occasionally. They will be cooked in a few minutes.

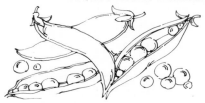

JACKET POTATOES

1 large potato per person

Other variations
2 tablespoons cottage cheese to
*   which is added:*
*   chopped parsley or*
1 tablespoon date and apple
*   chutney or*
1 tablespoon grated low fat cheese
and cayenne pepper or
1 tablespoon chopped celery

Scrub potato clean, leaving the skin on. Prick potato with a skewer in several places. Place potato in a piece of foil. Grind black pepper over and secure tightly in foil. Cook in a hot oven for 40 minutes or until potato is soft.

Remove from foil. Squeeze an opening in the top of the potato and add 2 tablespoons cottage cheese, to which you have added chopped chives.

PUMPKIN AU GRATIN

Serves 4

1 pound pumpkin
freshly ground black pepper
dash of nutmeg
1/4 teaspoon ground cloves
3 egg whites
1/4 cup skim milk
1/4 cup non-fat yogurt
1/2 cup finely grated low fat cheese

Peel and slice pumpkin, boil until tender and drain. Combine with pepper, nutmeg, cloves. Place in an ovenproof casserole. Beat egg whites, skim milk, yogurt and 1/4 cup grated cheese. Pour over pumpkin. Sprinkle over remaining cheese. Bake in hot oven for 15–20 minutes.

BAKED PUMPKIN WITH SESAME SEEDS

1 pound pumpkin
water to cover
yogurt
sesame seeds

Cut pumpkin into serving pieces. Steam pumpkin in water until just tender, then brush the top of each piece of pumpkin with natural yogurt and sprinkle with sesame seeds. Cook until pumpkin is tender and sesame seeds golden.

PUMPKIN FRITTERS

Serves 4

8 slices pumpkin (approximately
* 1 inch thick)*

Batter
1 cup wholemeal flour
1 teaspoon curry powder
1 teaspoon paprika
1 cup skim milk
2 egg whites
wholemeal breadcrumbs and sesame
* seeds*

Par boil pumpkin slices to tenderize slightly. Drain on paper towels. Mix together all the batter ingredients. Dip pumpkin slices into batter and then press into breadcrumbs and sesame seed mixture. Cook in a non-stick pan until the crumb mixture is golden brown. Turn and repeat on the other side.

Served with salad, this is an excellent dish for a quick lunch.

SPINACH ROLLS

Serves 6

1 pound spinach, cooked, finely
* shredded and drained*
6 wholemeal rolls
2 cups cottage cheese
3 egg whites
black pepper
¼ teaspoon nutmeg

Remove tops from rolls. Scoop out bread and make into breadcrumbs. Combine spinach, breadcrumbs, cottage cheese, egg whites, black pepper and nutmeg. Spoon mixture evenly into rolls and replace tops. Wrap in foil and cook in a moderately hot oven for 30 minutes. Serve with salad.

BAKED TOMATOES

Serves 4

2 large ripe tomatoes
1 cup wholemeal breadcrumbs
1 onion, finely chopped
1/2 teaspoon mixed herbs
2 tablespoons finely chopped green
   bell pepper
1/4 cup grated low fat cheese

Cut tomatoes in half. Remove seeds. Combine breadcrumbs, onion, herbs, bell pepper and cheese. Spoon mixture into tomatoes and bake in moderate oven for 20 minutes or until tomatoes are tender and filling is starting to brown.

ZUCCHINI BOATS

Serves 4

8 zucchini
1 onion, finely chopped
1 clove garlic, crushed
2 tomatoes, peeled, seeded and
   chopped
1 small red bell pepper, finely diced
1 teaspoon capers, chopped
1/2 teaspoon basil
1/2 teaspoon orange rind

Blanch zucchini in boiling water for 6 minutes. Drain. Halve carefully and scoop out seeds. Place in a flat ovenproof casserole. Combine onion, garlic, tomatoes, bell pepper, capers, basil and orange rind in a pan. Stir over low heat until mixture boils. Boil 1 minute. Remove from heat and spoon mixture into zucchini halves. Cook in a moderate oven for 15–20 minutes. Remove and cool slightly. Serve in lettuce leaves.

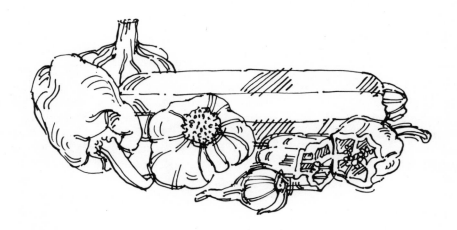

ZUCCHINI OMELETTE

Serves 1

3 egg whites, lightly beaten with a
  fork
1 small zucchini, grated
2 tablespoons parsley
2 tablespoons chives
black pepper to taste

Combine all ingredients and pour into a non-stick omelette pan. When mixture is firm, turn over and cook the other side. Serve on wholemeal toast or roll up and serve with a salad.

VEGETABLE CASSEROLE WITH ORANGE RUTABAGA SAUCE

Serves 6–8

4 large potatoes, peeled and cut into
  large cubes
2 carrots, cut into large chunks
1 parsnip, peeled and cut into
  chunks
1 cup celery chunks
1 cup green peas
1 cup green beans
2 cans tomato pieces, drained
1 green and 1 red bell pepper, cut
  into chunks
2 cups unsweetened orange juice
1 tablespoon orange rind
2 cups water, vegetable or chicken
  stock (see page 31 and 33)
2 cups grated rutabaga
black pepper to taste

Place all ingredients in a large earthenware casserole with the lid on. Cook in a moderately hot oven for 2 hours. This casserole is ready to eat when vegetables are tender and liquid has reduced into a thick sauce. If a thicker sauce is preferred, add a small amount of cornstarch dissolved in some of the cooled liquid.

R ICE

CARROT AND CUMIN RICE

Serves 4

4 cups cooked brown rice
2 cups grated raw carrot
1/2 cup currants
1/2 cup finely chopped green onions
1/2–1 teaspoon cumin
1/2–1 teaspoon ginger powder
1/4 cup unsweetened pineapple juice

Combine all ingredients and mix well. Serve.

CHILLI RICE

Serves 4

4 cups cooked brown rice
4 egg whites
1/2 cup soy milk or skim milk
1 cup finely chopped celery
1/2 cup finely chopped green onion
1 small green bell pepper, cut in
  strips
1 small red bell pepper, cut in strips
1/2 teaspoon dried basil
1/2 teaspoon ginger powder
1/2 teaspoon turmeric
1/2–1 teaspoon chilli powder
1/2 cup stock

Beat egg whites and soy milk. Very lightly grease a non-stick pan. Place pan over heat to get moderately hot. Pour over egg white mixture and let cook until it sets. Turn, cook other side. Remove from heat and slice thinly. Add celery, onion, bell peppers and spices to pan with stock. Cook for 2 minutes on high or until all moisture is absorbed. Add rice. Turn off heat. Toss rice through, to just warm. Add sliced egg white and serve.

LEMON HERBED RICE

Serves 4

4 cups cooked brown rice
1 cup of mixed fresh finely chopped
  herbs (parsley, chives, basil,
  oregano, tarragon, thyme)
2 tablespoons tarragon vinegar
2 teaspoons lemon juice
2 teaspoons lemon rind

Combine all ingredients and mix well. Serve.

SAFFRON RICE

Serves 2

1 cup long grain brown rice
2¹/₂ cups chicken stock
pinch of saffron
1 teaspoon lemon rind
¹/₄–¹/₂ teaspoon cinnamon

Bring stock to a boil and simmer. Add saffron. Leave for 3 minutes. Add rice. Cover and cook until soft but still slightly 'bitey', and rice has absorbed the color and flavor of the saffron. Add lemon rind and cinnamon. Mix well. Serve.

TABBOULEH RICE

Serves 6

2 cups cooked brown rice
4 tomatoes, peeled, seeded and finely
  chopped
4 green onions, finely chopped
1 cup finely chopped parsley
1 cup finely chopped fresh coriander
¹/₂ cup finely chopped fresh mint
³/₄ cup garlic vinaigrette (see
  page 56)

Combine all ingredients and mix well. Chill and serve.

Opposite:
Mushroom pizza (p82) Hawaiian pizza (p82)
Vegetarian pizza (p83)

VEGETABLE FRIED RICE

Serves 5

2 cups cooked cold brown rice
1 small green bell pepper, chopped
  finely
1 medium onion or 6 green onions,
  chopped
4 ounces mushrooms, sliced finely
1 medium carrot, grated
1 cup bean sprouts
1 cup finely shredded cabbage
black pepper to taste
1/4 teaspoon chilli powder
2 egg whites
chopped parsley

Moisten the base of a non-stick pan or wok. Slowly cook egg whites until well set, then chop. Add rice and vegetables. Cook on low heat for 10 minutes. Keep moving the ingredients so rice and vegetables do not stick. Stir through parsley just prior to serving.

SWEET RICE

Serves 8

4 cups cooked brown rice
1/4 cup dried apricots, finely chopped
1/4 cup currants
1/4 cup raisins, finely chopped
1/4 cup dried apples, finely chopped
1 medium sized carrot, diced
2 stalks celery, diced
1 tablespoon sunflower seeds
1 tablespoon sesame seeds, toasted
2 teaspoons orange rind, grated
1/4 cup unsweetened orange juice

Combine all ingredients and serve immediately.

Opposite:
Fruit salad combination (p108)
Apples baked with fruit filling (p103)
Lemon meringue pie (p109)

DESSERTS

APPLES BAKED WITH FRUIT FILLING

Serves 4

4 green apples
4 tablespoons dried fruit medley
1/2 teaspoon cinnamon
1/2 teaspoon mixed spice
rind of 1 orange, finely grated
1 cup unsweetened orange juice

Core apples and leave whole. Peel skin from the top half. Combine dried fruit, spices and orange rind. Fill apples with this mixture. Place in a pan that apples will stand up in. Pour over orange juice. Cover and simmer gently until apples are just tender (approximately 10–15 minutes). Serve with low fat cream, non-fat yogurt or custard.

BANANA CUSTARD

Serves 6–8

4 cups skim milk
1 cup cornstarch
2 teaspoons vanilla
1 tablespoon orange rind
1/4–1/2 cup apple juice concentrate
1 cup non-fat yogurt
3–4 bananas
1 tablespoon lemon juice

Bring 3 cups of milk to just below boiling. Combine 1 cup of milk, cornstarch, vanilla and orange rind and mix to make a paste. Add to milk and stir briskly until thick. Cook for 2 minutes, stirring continuously. Remove from heat. Add apple juice concentrate and mix well. Add yogurt and mix well.

Cut bananas into thin rounds and brush with lemon juice. Line a shallow baking dish with foil. Overlap banana pieces on base of dish. Pour over custard. Refrigerate to set for at least 3 hours. Turn out and cut into squares. Top with low fat cream.

Note: Rice flour can be substituted for cornstarch.

BANANA DATE STEAMED PUDDING

Serves 6–8

1 cup dates
1 cup raisins
1 teaspoon vanilla
2 small mashed bananas
1 cup plain wholemeal flour
1 teaspoon bicarbonate of soda
1 teaspoon baking powder
1 teaspoon cinnamon
1 teaspoon nutmeg
2 egg whites

'Whipped Ricotta Cream'

1 cup low fat ricotta cheese
3/4 cup natural unsweetened fruit
   juice, (apple, orange, pear, peach
   or apricot)
2 teaspoons vanilla

Custard

2 cups skim milk
2 tablespoons unsweetened orange
   juice
1 tablespoon vanilla
3 tablespoons arrowroot, cornstarch
   or rice flour

To make pudding Place dates and raisins in a food processor and mince finely. Add vanilla and bananas and mix well.

Sift the dry ingredients. Fold flour through the fruit mixture. Beat egg whites until stiff. Fold through mixture. Pour into a lightly greased pudding basin. Seal.

Place in a pan and fill to 1 1/2 inches from the top of pudding basin with boiling water. Keep just boiling for 1 1/2–1 3/4 hours. Serve with whipped ricotta cream or custard.

To make whipped cream Whip all ingredients until smooth. Chill.

To make custard Combine all ingredients and mix well. Bring slowly to a boil in a small pan. Stir continuously until the custard thickens.

CANTALOUPE BERRY BASKET

Serves 3

1 cantaloupe
2–3 cups mixed berries such as
   boysenberries, blueberries,
   loganberries, blackberries or
   strawberries

Cut cantaloupe into quarters. Remove seeds and scoop out the flesh to make a basket-like hollow. Use a sharp knife to remove the flesh carefully from one quarter, leaving approximately 1/4 inch orange flesh. Cut the flesh into pieces and give to children to nibble on while you make these fun baskets.

Cut the outer skin into three long strips which will become the basket handles. Attach these to either end of remaining pieces of cantaloupe, using toothpicks. Wash berries and drain. Fill baskets. Serve with homemade ice cream or non-fat yogurt.

BANANA MOUSSE

Serves 6

2 frozen bananas
1/4 cup lemon juice
3 cups low fat evaporated milk, well chilled
2 teaspoons vanilla
2 tablespoons gelatin
1/4 cup boiling water
3 egg whites
1/2–1 teaspoon nutmeg

Peel bananas and purée. Add lemon juice. Beat milk until thick and creamy. Fold through bananas. Add vanilla. Mix gelatin with boiling water. Fold through banana mixture. Beat egg whites until stiff. Fold through with nutmeg. Pour into a mold or individual glass goblets.

Serve with whipped cream and slices of fresh banana.

For special occasions, you might like to add 1 to 2 teaspoons of rum.

Note: To freeze bananas, place whole unpeeled bananas in freezer for at least 12 hours. To remove skins when frozen cut each banana into 4 pieces and then peel carefully.

BANANA YOGURT PIE

Serves 6

Base
2 cups rolled oats
1 cup dates
1 tablespoon vanilla
2 tablespoons unsweetened orange juice
2 tablespoons carob powder

Filling
2 frozen bananas, peeled and chopped
1 cup low fat evaporated skim milk
1/2 teaspoon vanilla
1 cup non-fat yogurt
1 tablespoon gelatin
1/4 cup boiling water

Topping
1 banana, thinly sliced
1/4 cup lemon juice
1 teaspoon nutmeg

To make base Combine base ingredients in a food processor and process until mixture begins to stick together (approximately 3 minutes). Do not over-process. Line a 9 inch pie dish with foil. Press mixture thinly around sides and base. Press down firmly. Refrigerate.

To make filling Pour the boiling water over the gelatin and stir to dissolve. Set aside to cool. Place frozen bananas in a food processor and process until smooth. Add milk. Process for a further 3 to 5 minutes, until thick and creamy and doubled in size. Add vanilla, yogurt and mix well. Add gelatin. Pour over base. Refrigerate until firm (at least 2 to 3 hours).

Soak the banana slices in lemon juice. Garnish the pie with the banana, then sprinkle over the nutmeg.

Note: For frozen bananas see Banana Mousse.

COLD CHRISTMAS PUDDING

Serves 10–12

4 ounces raisins
4 ounces dried apricots, finely
 chopped
4 ounces prunes, chopped
4 ounces currants
1 cup unsweetened orange juice
1 teaspoon mixed spice
2 tablespoons dry sherry
12 ounces cold cooked apple
1 tablespoon lemon juice
1/2 cup unsweetened apple juice
2 tablespoons gelatin
1/4 cup boiling water

Combine fruit, orange juice, mixed spice and sherry in a pan. Slowly bring to a boil. Simmer for 3 minutes. Remove from heat. Fold in apple. Combine lemon juice and apple juice. Dissolve gelatin in boiling water and add to apple and lemon juice. Pour over fruit and apple mixture and mix well. Spoon into a 6 cup capacity pudding mold.

Cover and refrigerate overnight or longer. Use a sharp knife to slice into portions.

VANILLA CREME

1 cup low fat ricotta cheese
3/4 cup unsweetened apple juice
1–2 teaspoons vanilla
2 teaspoons brandy

Whip all ingredients in a blender until smooth and chill.

FRUIT JELLIES

Fruit jellies are a delicious treat any time of the day. They are easily made from freshly squeezed fruit juices or bottled, unsweetened fruit juices. For interesting flavors try different juice combinations and add some freshly chopped fruit to the jelly just before it sets. I have used agar powder to set the fruit to make a jelly. You could easily substitute gelatin as the setting ingredient. If using agar the setting time is greatly reduced.

APPLE MINT JELLY

Serves 4

2 cups unsweetened apple juice
1 teaspoon agar powder
1–2 teaspoons fresh mint or
 spearmint, finely chopped

Boil 1 teaspoon of agar with 1 cup apple juice for 3 minutes or until agar has dissolved. Stir briskly into remaining cold juice. Stir continuously for 3 minutes. Stir in the mint. Refrigerate to set.

FRUIT COCKTAIL JELLY

Serves 4

2 cups unsweetened fruit cocktail
    juice (combination of orange,
    apple, mango)
1 teaspoon agar powder

Boil 1 teaspoon agar with 1 cup juice for 3 minutes or until agar is thoroughly dissolved. Stir briskly into remaining cold juice. Stir continuously for 3 minutes. Refrigerate to set. It will set very quickly.

BLUEBERRY GRAPE JELLY

Serves 6

2 cups dark unsweetened grape juice
2 teaspoons agar powder
2 cups blueberries, fresh or frozen

Boil 2 teaspoons agar with 1 cup juice and blueberries for 3 minutes or until agar has dissolved. Stir briskly into remaining cold juice. Stir continuously for 3 minutes. Refrigerate to set.

PINEAPPLE JELLY

Serves 4–6

3/4 cup unsweetened pineapple juice
1 cup water
1 can unsweetened pineapple pieces
1 1/2 teaspoons agar powder

Boil 1 1/2 teaspoons agar with 1 cup water for 3 minutes or until agar has dissolved. Stir briskly into the pineapple juice. Stir continuously for 3 minutes. Chop pineapple pieces roughly. Fold pineapple through just before jelly sets.

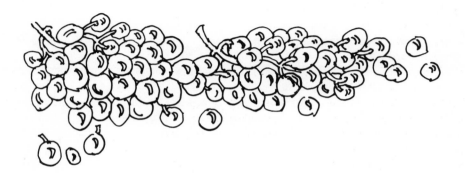

RAINBOW WOBBLY JELLY

Serves 4–6

Orange
2 cups unsweetened orange juice
1 teaspoon agar

Purple
2 cups unsweetened dark grape juice
1 teaspoon agar

Clear
2 cups unsweetened apple juice
1 teaspoon agar

Make up jellies separately using basic jelly-making instructions. Pour into separate containers. Leave jelly to set. Cut into squares. Spoon into parfait glasses, alternating colors.

FRUIT SALAD COMBINATIONS

Fruit salad can be a nutritious finish to a meal, served for breakfast or as a snack meal. It need never become boring if you change the combinations of the fruit and soak it in a little juice. Serve plain, with homemade ice cream, custard or non-fat yogurt.

- Orange segments, grapefruit segments, pineapple chunks and orange juice
- Strawberries, watermelon balls and sparkling apple juice
- Cantaloupe balls, honeydew melon balls, green grapes, grated fresh ginger root and natural, unsweetened pear juice
- Banana chunks, pineapple chunks, apple chunks, purple grapes, lemon juice and natural, unsweetened apple juice
- Honeydew melon chunks, cantaloupe chunks, pineapple chunks, purple and green grapes, blueberries and dark grape juice
- Orange chunks, apple chunks, pear chunks, pineapple chunks, strips of dried apricot and orange or apple juice
- Apricot halves, peach pieces, nectarine pieces and apricot nectar
- Pineapple chunks, banana chunks and unsweetened pineapple juice
- Strawberries, kiwi fruit chunks, green grapes, grated orange and lemon rind and unsweetened orange juice
- Bananas sliced, kiwi fruit sliced, pineapple wedges, orange segments, water chestnuts thinly sliced, lemon and orange juice
- Mango, pineapple, fine strips of dried apricot (optional) and unsweetened orange juice
- Dark plum halves, blueberries, purple grapes and dark grape juice
- Watermelon balls, honeydew melon balls, cantaloupe balls, sparkling apple juice and lemon juice
- Mango, pineapple and orange chunks and fresh halved dates

GINGER PEARS

Serves 6

6 pears
1 1/2 cups apple juice
1 inch piece fresh ginger, peeled
2 teaspoons finely grated lemon rind

Peel pears, leaving stems on. Place in a pan so they all stand up. Pour over apple juice. Add a piece of ginger and lemon rind. Simmer until pears are soft, but do not overcook. Remove from heat. Cover and leave until cold.

Place in a serving bowl. Remove ginger. Refrigerate. Serve chilled with small amount of juice.

LEMON MERINGUE PIE

Serves 8

Pastry
1 cup wholemeal plain flour
1 cup rolled oats
1/4 cup cold pressed oil
2 tablespoons apple juice
  concentrate
4 tablespoons lemon juice

Lemon filling
3/4 cup lemon juice
1/2 cup apple juice concentrate
grated rind of 1 orange
  (approximately
  1 tablespoon)
grated rind of 1 lemon
  (approximately
  1 tablespoon)
1 1/4 cups water
1/2 cup cornstarch

Meringue topping
4 egg whites
3 ounces almonds, finely ground
1 teaspoon vanilla
2 tablespoons apple juice
  concentrate

Combine all ingredients in a food processor and process until pastry binds together. Roll out to fit a small fluted pie dish. Cook at 450°F for 10–15 minutes. Cool.

Place the first 4 ingredients for the lemon filling plus 1 cup water in a small pan and bring to a boil. Combine 1/4 cup water with cornstarch and make into a paste. Stir into lemon mixture, stirring continuously as it boils and thickens. Cook for 2 minutes. Cool slightly. Pour into base and leave to set.

The lemon filling should be quite cold and firm before the meringue topping is added.

Beat egg whites until stiff peaks form. Add all other ingredients separately, mixing well after each addition. Spoon over lemon filling. Cook at 400°F for 10–15 minutes or until top has browned.

This pie should be kept out of the refrigerator for best flavor. Serve with non-fat frozen yogurt or homemade ice cream.

109

LEMON PEAR SORBET

Serves 8–10

20 ounce can unsweetened pears
  and juice
1/4 cup apple juice concentrate
4 tablespoons lemon juice

Purée all ingredients. Pour into an ice cream maker and follow freezing instructions. Serve in sugar-free ice cream cones. Garnish with a piece of fresh fruit such as a strawberry.

PANCAKES

Makes 16 pancakes

4 cups water
3 cups rolled oats
2 cups wholemeal plain flour
2 teaspoons baking powder
1/2 cup apple juice concentrate
2 teaspoons vanilla
4 egg whites

Combine all ingredients except egg whites in a food blender or processor. (It may be easier to divide quantity into 2 and do in separate batches.) Process until smooth. Beat egg whites until stiff peaks form. Fold egg whites through the mixture.

Cook pancakes on a hot non-stick flat pan. Approximately 1/2 cup of mixture makes 1 pancake. As air bubbles appear turn over and brown other side. Move pancake mixture around to spread for an even texture. Keep pancakes hot in the oven by placing between two pieces of foil on a baking tray. Set oven at approximately 200°F. When ready to serve, fold pancakes in half. Top with a scoop of homemade ice cream and a topping of your choice, or with fresh fruit such as sliced strawberries, mashed bananas or pineapple.

Or

Make a pancake stack. Pour sauce over the top and let it dribble down over the edges.

LEMON TOPPING

3/4 cup lemon juice
1/2 cup apple juice concentrate
1/2 teaspoon orange extract
rind of 1 orange, grated (optional)
1 1/4 cups water
1/4 cup cornstarch

Combine first 4 ingredients plus 1 cup of water in a small pan. Combine 1/4 cup water and cornstarch to make a paste. Slowly bring lemon mixture to a boil. Add cornstarch mixture and stir continuously until sauce thickens. Remove from heat and cool slightly. Pour over homemade ice cream and pancakes.

BLUEBERRY TOPPING

2 cups unsweetened natural pear
  juice
1/3 cup apple juice concentrate
12 ounces blueberries, fresh or
  frozen
1 tablespoon lemon juice
1/4 cup cornstarch

Mix 1/4 cup pear juice with cornstarch to make a paste. Combine other ingredients in a small pan and slowly bring to a boil. Add cornstarch and stir continuously until sauce thickens. Remove from heat and cool slightly. Pour over homemade ice cream and pancakes.

BANANA TOPPING

1 banana per pancake
1 1/2 cups unsweetened orange, pear
  or apple juice
1 tablespoon lemon juice
1 tablespoon apple juice concentrate
1–2 teaspoons cornstarch

Add a little juice to cornstarch to make a paste. Add remaining liquid to a pan and bring to a boil. Turn heat down and simmer until liquid reduces slightly. Slice bananas and add to the sauce. Bring to a boil and cook for 1 minute. Add cornstarch and stir until sauce boils and thickens. Pour over pancakes and top with ricotta low fat whipped cream.

CHERRY TOPPING

1 pound pitted cherries
1 cup unsweetened orange juice
1/2 cup apple juice concentrate
1/2 teaspoon orange extract
grated rind of 1 lemon
1 tablespoon lemon juice
1 teaspoon (scant) agar

Place all ingredients except cherries in a pan. Bring to a boil and simmer for 10–15 minutes to dissolve agar. Add cherries and cook a further 5 minutes. Remove from heat and cool slightly. Pour over pancakes and top with ricotta low fat whipped cream.

Note: Any leftover toppings can be refrigerated and used as a homemade sugar-free spread.

RICOTTA LOW FAT WHIPPED CREAM

Beat low fat ricotta cheese until smooth. Flavor with 1–2 teaspoons of vanilla and thin to desired consistency with unsweetened natural fruit juice such as pear or apple juice, or apricot nectar.

PINEAPPLE YOGURT PIE

Serves 8

Base

1 cup dried mixed fruit
1¹/₂ cups rolled oats
¹/₂ cup almonds in their skins
1 teaspoon vanilla
¹/₄ cup unsweetened orange juice

Filling

1 tablespoon gelatin
¹/₄ cup boiling water
1 cup finely chopped fresh or bottled
  pineapple
¹/₄ cup pineapple juice
1 teaspoon grated lemon rind
¹/₃ cup apple juice concentrate
2 cups non-fat yogurt

Topping

thinly sliced fresh pineapple

To make base Combine ingredients and process until mixture begins to stick together (approximately 3 to 5 minutes). Do not overprocess. Line a 9 inch pie dish with foil. Press mixture thinly around sides and base. Press down firmly. Refrigerate.

To make filling Pour the boiling water over the gelatin and stir to dissolve. Combine pineapple, pineapple juice, lemon rind and apple juice concentrate in a food processor and lightly process to combine. Add yogurt and mix well. Add gelatin. Pour over base. Refrigerate until firm (at least 2 to 3 hours).
  Garnish the top with thinly sliced pineapple.

PUMPKIN AND NUT PIE

Serves 8–10

Base

¹/₂ cup almonds in their skins
¹/₄ cup raisins
1 cup wheat flakes or rolled oats
1¹/₂ teaspoons cinnamon
1 tablespoon apple juice

Filling

1 pound cooked pumpkin
2 tablespoon apple juice concentrate
2 teaspoons finely grated orange
  rind
¹/₂ cup soy milk or skim milk
1 tablespoon vanilla
¹/₂ cup currants or finely chopped
  dried apricots
4 egg whites

To make base Combine all base ingredients in a food processor and process until it just begins to stick together. Line a 9 inch pie dish with foil and press mixture very thinly over base and sides.

To make filling Place pumpkin, apple juice concentrate, orange rind, soy milk and vanilla in a food processor and process until smooth. Fold in currants. Beat egg whites until quite stiff and fold in. Pour into base and cook at 350°F for 50 minutes. Serve chilled topped with whipped cream and a shake of nutmeg.

PEACH YOGURT MOUSSE

20 ounce can peaches, unsweetened
and drained
2 tablespoons apple juice
concentrate
1/2 teaspoon orange extract
1 tablespoon gelatin
3 tablespoons boiling water
1 1/2–2 cups non-fat yogurt

Blend peaches, apple juice concentrate and orange extract. Dissolve gelatin in boiling water and add to peach mixture. Fold in yogurt. Pour into a wet mold and refrigerate until set. Serve with fresh strawberries and slices of fresh peaches.

STRAWBERRY CUSTARD TARTS

Makes 8 small tarts

2 cups strawberries

Pastry
1 cup wholemeal plain flour
1 cup rolled oats
1/4 cup cold pressed oil
2 tablespoons apple juice
concentrate
2–4 tablespoons unsweetened
orange juice

Lightly grease 8 small foil (3 x 1 1/2 inch) pie plates. Combine all ingredients for pastry in a food processor. Using the steel blade, process until pastry binds together. Cut pastry into 8 equal pieces and roll out to fit the pie plates. Trim edges and place on a baking tray. Cook at 400°F for 10 minutes. Cool.

Custard Use the same ingredients as are used in the recipe for *banana custard*. Halve all quantities except orange rind. Cook using the same method and leave to cool slightly.

Pour custard into shells. You should have approximately 1/4 cup custard left over for children and adults who love to lick the bowl. Refrigerate. Decorate the tops with fresh strawberries.

WINTER FRUIT SALAD

Serves 4–6

1/2 cup fresh dates, halved and pitted
1/2 cup prunes, halved and pitted
1/2 cup dried figs, stalks removed
* and halved*
1/3 cup whole unblanched almonds
1/4 cup walnut halves
1 cup unsweetened orange juice and
* 1 teaspoon cinnamon*
1/2 cup seedless grapes
1 orange, peeled and segmented
2 small cantaloupes for serving
* (optional)*

Combine dried fruits and nuts and place in a clean jar. Pour the liquid over them. Shake to coat the fruit with the liquid. Allow to soak for at least 4 hours. Can be stored for several weeks. Store in the refrigerator.

Remove small amount of flesh from cleaned and halved cantaloupes. Spoon fruit mixture, leaving enough space to add grapes and orange segments, into cantaloupes.

Serve a bowl of homemade vanilla ice cream to complement this salad. Eat the fruits and serve ice cream in the cantaloupe to absorb all the delicious juices that remain, or serve the ice cream in goblets, after the dessert has been eaten, as a cool refreshment at the end of the meal.

WINTER PEARS

Serves 6

6 pears
2 cups unsweetened dark grape juice
2 teaspoons finely grated orange
* rind*
2 teaspoons arrowroot
1/4 cup water

Peel pears, leaving stems on. Pour the grape juice into a large pan, and stand pears upright in it. Cover and simmer until pears are tender. Remove from heat and leave for 1 hour covered. Remove pears carefully to individual serving bowls. Return juice to heat and slowly bring to a boil. Stir in arrowroot (to which the water has been added to make a paste). Turn off heat. Stir briskly as it thickens. Pour a small amount over each pear.

ICE CREAMS

An ice cream maker will make the best non-fat ice cream without added sugar, egg yolks or artificial flavorings and colorings. There are many different designs now available so it is necessary to choose wisely and follow the manufacturer's instructions on ice cream freezing times.

The cheapest or the most expensive machine is not necessarily the best machine for you. Consider how many members of your family enjoy ice cream treats, and how often you would use the machine. Add up how much money you would spend over a 12 month period on commercial ice cream, then decide on whether an ice cream maker is a worthwhile investment for your family.

I personally think that the greatest advantage of such an investment is knowing what ingredients your ice cream contains. The endless varieties of ice cream you can make and all the wonderful flavors are just an added bonus!

MAKING ICE CREAM WITHOUT AN ICE CREAM MAKER

- All ingredients used should be ice cold.
- All equipment used should be well chilled. Place in freezer for at least 15 minutes prior to using.
- Pour ice cream into well chilled metal freezing containers.
- To avoid ice cream texture becoming icy rather than creamy, you will need to rebeat it several times, just as icicles begin to appear around the edges again, making sure that all equipment is well chilled.
- This ice cream does not store well as it becomes rock hard. Make small batches and eat as required.
- Should ice cream become too hard, place in a chilled blender or food processor and quickly blend to a creamy texture. Eat immediately.

VANILLA ICE CREAM

Makes 3–4 quarts

1 can low-fat evaporated milk, well
  chilled
6 tablespoons skim milk powder
1 cup non-fat yogurt
1/2 tablespoon vanilla

Combine all ingredients in a large bowl and beat for 3 minutes. Place in the freezer for 40 minutes until well chilled and starting to ice up. Remove from freezer and beat until creamy, thick and double in size. Pour into ice cream trays and freeze.

RICH CREAMY CUSTARD ICE CREAM

Serves 10

4 cups skim milk
1/4 cup cornstarch
1 tablespoon orange rind
2 teaspoons vanilla
1/2 cup apple juice concentrate
1 cup non-fat yogurt or extra skim
  milk

Place 3 cups milk in a pan and slowly bring to the boil. Combine cornstarch, grated orange rind and vanilla with 1 cup milk. Stir to make a smooth paste. Add to milk and stir continuously for 2–3 minutes until the mixture thickens. Remove from heat. Add apple juice concentrate and fold through. Add yogurt or milk and stir again until smooth. Cool until just warm. Pour into ice cream maker and follow freezing instructions.

LIGHT CAROB ICE CREAM

Serves 6

12 ounce can ice cold evaporated
  skim milk
or
3 cups non-fat yogurt
1 tablespoon carob powder
2 teaspoons vanilla
2 tablespoons apple juice
  concentrate

If using milk, beat until thick and at least doubled in size. Combine carob, vanilla and apple juice concentrate. Add to milk or yogurt. If using yogurt fold through. Do not beat or you will lose the creamy texture. Pour into ice cream maker and follow freezing instructions.

Opposite:
Winter pears (p114)

RICH CREAMY CAROB ICE CREAM

Serves 6

12 ounce can ice cold evaporated skim milk
1/4 cup unsweetened carob powder
1/4 cup apple juice concentrate
2 teaspoons vanilla

Beat milk until thick and at least doubled in size. Combine carob, apple juice concentrate and vanilla to make a thick paste. Add this mixture to milk while still beating. Pour into the ice cream maker and follow freezing instructions.

Variations   Add 2 tablespoons finely chopped roasted almonds, toasted coconut or finely chopped raisins.

BANANA ICE CREAM

1 banana = 1 serve

Place whole unpeeled bananas in the freezer overnight. Remove from freezer and carefully remove the peel. Cut banana into 4 pieces. Place into a food processor and, using the steel blade, process until thick and creamy. Eat immediately, scooped onto your favorite fruit.

Variation   For every banana used add 1/4 cup yogurt, 1 teaspoon lemon juice and 1/2 teaspoon vanilla. Process as above. Pour mixture into a well chilled metal bowl and freeze for 1–2 hours. Scoop into sugar free ice cream cones.

STRAWBERRY ICE CREAM

Serves 8 –10

12 ounce can ice cold evaporated skim milk
2 teaspoons vanilla
1 tablespoon apple juice concentrate
2 baskets strawberries

Beat milk until thick and creamy and at least doubled in size. Add vanilla and apple juice concentrate. Mash 1 basket of strawberries and cut remaining strawberries in half. Add strawberries. Pour into ice cream maker and follow freezing instructions.

Opposite:
Strawberry ice cream cake (p118)

CHUNKY BANANA ICE CREAM

Serves 8 –10

12 can ice cold evaporated skim
   milk
3 teaspoons vanilla
2 tablespoons lemon juice
4 bananas

Beat milk until thick and creamy and at least doubled in size. Add vanilla and lemon juice. Add roughly chopped bananas and beat lightly. Pour into ice cream maker and follow freezing instructions.

ORANGE FLAVORED ICE CREAM

Serves 6

12 ounce can ice cold evaporated
   skim milk
2 teaspoons vanilla
1 teaspoon orange extract
1/4 cup apple juice concentrate

Beat milk until thick and at least doubled in size. Add remaining ingredients while still beating. Pour into ice cream maker and follow freezing instructions.

STRAWBERRY ICE CREAM CAKE

Serves 8 –10

1 quart of homemade vanilla ice
   cream
3 baskets of strawberries, washed
   and hulled
1/2 cup toasted almond flakes
whole fresh strawberries for
   decoration

Make vanilla ice cream, but do not freeze in the final step. Pour 1/3 of the ice cream into a foil lined round pan. Slice strawberries finely and use half in a layer on top of the ice cream mixture. Pour over 1/2 of remaining ice cream mixture, another layer of strawberries, then the remaining ice cream and freeze.

   To serve, turn out of pan, remove foil and place on a serving plate. Sprinkle over toasted flaked almonds and decorate the edge of the strawberry cake with fresh whole strawberries.

BOYSENBERRY ICE CREAM

Serves 8

8 ounce pack frozen unsweetened
  boysenberries
2 tablespoons apple juice
  concentrate
1 teaspoon vanilla
  or 1/2 teaspoon orange extract
1 1/2 cups evaporated skim milk
  or 8 ounce pack soy milk

Crush berries with the palm of your hand. Place in a blender or food processor. Process until icy. Pour in remaining ingredients. Beat until at least doubled in size. Pour into ice cream maker and follow freezing instructions.

FROZEN YOGURT POPSICLES

Strawberry
1 cup fresh strawberries, mashed
1–2 tablespoons apple juice
  concentrate (optional)
1/4 teaspoon orange extract
2 cups non-fat yogurt

Mix all ingredients thoroughly and spoon into popsicle molds.

Banana
1 cup mashed bananas
1 tablespoon lemon juice
1 teaspoon vanilla
2 cups non-fat yogurt

As above.

Pineapple crunch yogurt
1 tablespoon lemon juice
or
1/2 teaspoon orange extract
2 cups non-fat yogurt
1 cup unsweetened crushed
  pineapple

As above.

Carob peppermint
1 tablespoon carob powder
1 tablespoon boiling water
1/2 teaspoon peppermint flavoring
1/2 teaspoon vanilla
1 tablespoon apple juice
  concentrate
2 cups non-fat yogurt

Combine carob powder and boiling water to dissolve carob. Mix all ingredients thoroughly and pour into popsicle molds.

PINEAPPLE FLAVORED ICE CREAM

Serves 10–12

*12 ounce can ice cold evaporated
 skim milk*
2 teaspoons vanilla
2 cups unsweetened pineapple juice
1/2 cup apple juice concentrate

Beat milk until thick and at least doubled in size. Add remaining ingredients while still beating. Pour into ice cream maker and follow freezing instructions.

CAKES, MUFFINS AND SCONES

APRICOT AND BRAN MUFFINS

Makes 24

1 cup cooked apricots, drained
2¹/2 cups plain wholemeal flour,
   sifted
¹/2 cup bran
1 tablespoon baking powder
³/4 cup non-fat yogurt
2 teaspoons vanilla
¹/4 cup orange juice
4 egg whites

Purée apricots in a food processor. Combine dry ingredients and sift. Add to the food processor and blend just a little. Add yogurt and vanilla. Blend to incorporate. Add orange juice.

Beat egg whites until stiff. Add mixture to egg whites and fold in. Place spoonfuls in lightly oiled muffin trays.

Bake at 400°F for 25 minutes. Serve hot from the oven with apricot jam (see page 135). These are much tastier eaten hot rather than cold.

APRICOT LOAF

Makes 10 –12 slices

1 cup bran
1 cup dried apricots, chopped
³/4 cup dried nectarines or peaches,
   finely chopped
2 cups skim milk
1¹/2 cups wholemeal plain flour
¹/2 cup unbleached white flour
2 teaspoons baking powder

Mix bran, dried fruit and milk together in a bowl. Cover and let stand for at least 2 hours.

Sift the flours and baking powder. Add small amounts of flour to the apricot mixture and mix well. Pour mixture into a 9 inch x 5 inch lined, non-stick loaf pan and bake at 350°F for 45–60 minutes or until firm to touch or tap and an inserted skewer comes out dry.

BANANA CAROB MUFFINS

Makes 12

1 3/4 cups wholemeal plain flour
3 tablespoons carob powder
3 teaspoons baking powder
1 teaspoon cinnamon
1 teaspoon mixed spice
1 cup mashed banana
1/2 cup apple juice concentrate
1/4 cup cold pressed oil
1/4 cup non-fat yogurt
2 teaspoons vanilla
3 egg whites

Topping
2 heaped tablespoons rolled oats
1/2 teaspoon cinnamon
1 tablespoon apple juice concentrate

Sift dry ingredients twice. Combine banana, apple juice concentrate, oil, yogurt and vanilla. Add to flour and beat well. Beat egg whites until stiff peaks form. Fold in egg whites. Spoon into a lightly greased and floured muffin tray. Add cinnamon to rolled oats. Sprinkle over top of each muffin. Add just a drop of the apple juice concentrate. Cook at 350°F for 20–25 minutes.

BLUEBERRY MUFFINS

Makes approximately 12 large muffins

These are deliciously moist muffins that are best eaten warm, without adding any spreads

2 cups wholemeal plain flour
2 teaspoons baking powder
6 ounces fresh blueberries
1/4 cup cold pressed almond oil or grapeseed oil
1/2 cup apple juice concentrate
1/4 cup non-fat yogurt
2 teaspoons vanilla
2 egg whites

Sift flour and baking powder. Add blueberries and coat well with flour. Mix together oil, apple juice concentrate, yogurt and vanilla. Make a well in the center of the flour and pour in half the mixture. Gently combine without squashing blueberries. Add remaining mixture.

Beat egg whites until stiff. Gently fold egg whites through the blueberry mixture until just combined. Spoon mixture into a lightly oiled muffin tray. Cook at 350°F for 25–30 minutes. Remove from oven and eat while still warm.

CARROT AND PINEAPPLE MUFFINS

Makes approximately 24

1 cup wholemeal plain flour
1 cup unbleached white flour
2½ teaspoons baking powder
1 teaspoon mixed spice or
  ½ teaspoon nutmeg and
  ½ teaspoon cinnamon
3 ounces carrot, finely grated
3 ounces fresh pineapple, finely
  chopped (if using canned
  pineapple make sure it has no
  added sugar and drain it well)
½ cup raisins, finely chopped
½ cup apple juice concentrate
⅓ cup non-fat buttermilk
2 teaspoons vanilla
¼ cup cold pressed oil
2 egg whites

Sift dry ingredients twice. Add carrot, pineapple and raisins and coat well with flour. Combine apple juice concentrate, buttermilk, vanilla and oil. Add to flour mixture and mix well. Beat egg whites until stiff peaks form. Fold through the mixture. Spoon into a muffin tray. Cook at 350°F for 20–25 minutes.

CARROT CAKE WITH LEMON CHEESE TOPPING

Serves 12

2 cups carrot, finely grated
1 cup raisins
1½ teaspoons cinnamon
½ cup unsweetened orange juice
½ cup apple juice concentrate
⅓ cup cold pressed oil
1 cup wholemeal plain flour
1 cup unbleached white flour
3 teaspoons baking powder
2 egg whites

Lemon cheese topping
1 cup cold lemon topping
3 ounces low fat ricotta cheese

Place carrot, raisins, cinnamon, orange juice and apple juice concentrate in a pan and gently bring to a boil. Simmer for approximately 5–7 minutes or until raisins are soft. Remove from heat and leave to get cold. Add the oil and mix well. Combine the sifted flours and baking powder with the carrot mixture, mixing well. Beat egg whites until stiff and gently fold through the mixture. Spoon into a lined ring pan. Cook at 350°F for 45–50 minutes.

Cake should be completely cool before adding the topping.

Blend ingredients until smooth and refrigerate until topping is quite firm. Spread evenly over the top of the cake.

CHRISTMAS CAKE

This is a large cake (approximately 5 pounds) and is best made and eaten immediately. If you wish to store it, wrap it well and freeze, or keep in an airtight container in refrigerator. It contains no oils, egg yolks, sugar or butter.

4 ounces dried apricots
4 ounces raisins
4 ounces mixed orange and lemon
  peel
4 ounces currants
8 ounces prunes
8 ounces dates
2 tablespoons brandy and/or
  unsweetened orange juice to make
  1 cup liquid
2 ounces almonds in their skins
  (optional)
2 cups mashed pumpkin
1/2 cup apple juice concentrate
4 cups wholemeal plain flour
4 teaspoons baking powder
2 teaspoons baking soda
1 teaspoon cinnamon
1 teaspoon allspice
1/2 teaspoon nutmeg
6 egg whites
1 tablespoon vanilla

Chop fruits and soak in brandy and orange juice, covered, overnight. Roughly chop almonds and add to the fruit. Add pumpkin and apple juice concentrate. Mix well. Sift all the dry ingredients, twice. Fold flour into the fruit mixture in three parts and mix well. Beat egg whites until stiff. Gently fold egg whites through cake mixture. Add vanilla.

Prepare a 9 inch x 3 inch deep round cake pan with non-stick baking paper. Cut a long strip of brown paper, approximately 4 inches wide. Secure it around the top of the pan so that approximately 3 inches of brown paper is above the pan. Pour cake mixture into pan and spread evenly. Decorate with whole almonds if desired.

Cook at 350°F for 2 1/2–3 hours. Test after 2 1/2 hours with a fine skewer. Remove from oven. Cover with brown paper and dish cloth to keep the moisture in the cake. When cool, wrap in foil or plastic and keep in sealed container.

CINNAMON AND OATMEAL MUFFINS

Makes approximately 16

3/4 cup plain flour
2 teaspoons baking powder
2 teaspoons cinnamon
1 1/2 cups rolled oats
4 egg whites
1/2 cup evaporated milk (low fat)
1/2 cup non-fat yogurt
1 tablespoon apple juice concentrate
2 teaspoons orange rind, finely grated
1 teaspoon vanilla
1 cup apple, freshly grated

Sift flour, baking powder and cinnamon. Add rolled oats and mix together. Beat egg whites, add milk, yogurt, apple juice concentrate, orange rind and vanilla. Mix well. Add to flour and fold in. Add grated apple and mix well. Lightly grease muffin trays and sprinkle with bran. Shake off excess. Spoon mixture into muffin trays.

Cook at 350°F for 25–30 minutes.

BANANA AND DATE MUFFINS

Makes 12 monster muffins

2 1/2 cups oat bran
1 1/2 cups wholemeal flour
6 teaspoons baking powder
2 teaspoons mixed spice
1 teaspoon cinnamon
1 pound finely chopped banana
4 ounces finely chopped dates
1/2 cup apple juice concentrate
1/2 cup cold pressed grapeseed oil
1 cup evaporated skim milk
3 egg whites

Place oat bran in a bowl. Sift the next 4 ingredients over the oat bran. Mix flour and spices with oat bran. Add banana and dates to flour and toss well to break up and coat with flour. Combine apple concentrate, grapeseed oil and milk and combine with flour and oat mixture. Beat egg whites until soft and gently fold into the mixture. Spoon into lightly oiled and oat branned muffin tray. Mixture will come up over the top of tray. Cook at 350°F for 25–30 minutes. Remove from muffin tray and place on a wire rack to cool. Cover with a dishcloth.

BLUEBERRY OAT MUFFINS

Makes 12 monster muffins

2 cups oat bran
2 cups unbleached white flour
6 teaspoons baking powder
1 teaspoon cinnamon
1 teaspoon mixed spice
1/3 teaspoon ginger
1 pound blueberries (fresh or frozen
 – not canned)
1/2 cup cold pressed grapeseed oil
1/2 cup apple juice concentrate
1 cup non-fat or low fat buttermilk
2 teaspoons vanilla
3 egg whites

Sift the flour, baking powder, cinnamon, mixed spice and ginger over the oat bran, and mix together. Add the blueberries and coat well with flour. Combine the next four ingredients and fold into the flour and fruit mixture. Try not to squash the blueberries. Beat egg whites until stiff and gently fold into the mixture. Spoon into lightly oiled and floured muffin tray. Cook at 350°F for 25–30 minutes. Remove immediately and place on a wire rack to cool. Cover with a dishcoth.

FRESH PEAR AND CINNAMON MUFFINS

Makes 12 monster muffins

1 cup rolled oats
2 cups oat bran
1 cup unbleached white flour
6 teaspoons baking powder
3 teaspoons cinnamon
1/4 cup lemon juice
3/4 cup unsweetened orange juice
1/2 cup apple juice concentrate
1/2 cup cold pressed grapeseed oil
2 teaspoons vanilla
1 pound pears, cored and diced
3 egg whites

Combine rolled oats and oat bran. Sift the next three ingredients over the oats and combine. Combine the next six ingredients in a large bowl. Slowly fold in the dry ingredients, mixing well. Beat egg whites until stiff peaks form and gently fold in. Spoon into lightly oiled and oat branned muffin tray. Mixture will come up over the top of the tray. Cook at 350°F for 25–30 minutes. Remove from muffin tray and place on a wire rack to cool. Cover with a dishcloth.

CORNMEAL AND CURRANT BRAN MUFFINS

Makes 12 monster muffins

2 cups cornmeal
2 cups oat bran
6 teaspoons baking powder
1 cup currants
1 cup non-fat or low fat yogurt
1 cup skim milk
1/2 cup apple juice concentrate
1/2 cup cold pressed grapeseed oil
2 teaspoons vanilla
3 egg whites

Combine the first four ingredients and mix well. Combine all remaining ingredients except egg whites, then add to the cornmeal and oat mixture. Beat egg whites lightly and add to above. Spoon into lightly oiled and oat branned muffin tray. Cook at 350°F for 20–25 minutes. Remove from muffin tray and place on a wire rack to cool. Cover with a dishcloth.

HERB SCONES

Makes approximately 10

2 cups unbleached white flour
3 teaspoons baking powder
1 tablespoon fresh chives, finely
   chopped
1 tablespoon fresh parsley, finely
   chopped
1 tablespoon fresh rosemary or basil,
   finely chopped
2 tablespoons non-fat yogurt
good squeeze of lemon juice
   (approximately 1 tablespoon)
cup skim milk or soy milk

Sift flour and baking powder. Add herbs and coat with flour. Add yogurt and lemon juice and mix through until flour resembles fine breadcrumbs. Add milk and mix through, using a knife. Place scone dough on a lightly floured bench and knead lightly. Cut into desired shapes. Place on a non-stick baking tray. Cook at 400°F for 10–15 minutes.

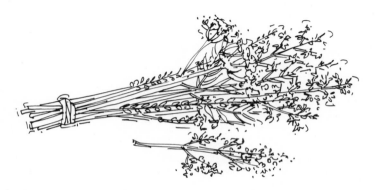

PUMPKIN WHOLEMEAL SCONES

Makes approximately 10

1 cup wholemeal plain flour
1 cup unbleached white flour
4 teaspoons baking powder
1 teaspoon nutmeg
2 tablespoons non-fat yogurt
good squeeze of lemon juice
   (approximately 1 tablespoon)
2 teaspoons apple juice concentrate
1/2 cup lightly packed raw pumpkin,
   grated
cup skim milk

Sift dry ingredients twice. Add pumpkin and toss in flour to coat well. Add yogurt, lemon juice and apple juice concentrate. Use a knife to mix together. Slowly add milk, still using the knife to bind ingredients. The mixture will be slightly sticky.

Scrape from bowl onto a lightly floured board. Knead gently. Too much kneading will make the scones heavy. Cut into desired shapes. Place on a non-stick scone tray. Cook at 425°F for 10–12 minutes.

ZUCCHINI CURRANT CAKE

2¹/2 cups wholemeal plain flour
2 teaspoons baking powder
1 teaspoon baking soda
1 teaspoon cinnamon
1 teaspoon mixed spice
1/4 cup cold pressed almond oil
1/2 cup non-fat yogurt
1 tablespoon natural maple syrup
2 cups raw zucchini, grated
1 cup currants
4 egg whites

Sift dry ingredients. Combine oil, yogurt, maple syrup and mix well. Add zucchini and currants. Mix again. Fold in flour. Beat egg whites until stiff peaks form. Gently fold them in the fairly stiff zucchini mixture. Turn it into a foil lined, deep sided, 8 inch square pan.

Cook at 350°F for 1 hour. Cover with foil for 10 minutes. Remove foil and leave in pan to cool.

HEALTH MUNCHIES, BARS AND SLICES

APRICOT AND ALMOND HEALTH CHEWS

1/2 cup dried apricots, chopped
1/4 cup unsweetened orange juice
2 tablespoons apple juice
* concentrate*
1/2 cup skim milk powder
1/4 cup whole almonds, roughly
* chopped*
1 tablespoon sesame seeds, toasted
1 teaspoon orange rind, grated
1/2 cup currants
1/4 cup flake coconut
extra flake coconut, toasted

Place apricots, orange juice and apple juice concentrate in a pan and simmer over low heat for 10 minutes. Do not drain. Remove pan from heat. Blend in skim milk powder. Add almonds, sesame seeds, grated orange rind, currants and coconut. Mix well and leave to cool slightly.

Roll mixture into a log shape and roll in toasted coconut. Roll up in foil and keep in refrigerator. Cut into rounds as required. Wrap individual pieces in colored cellophane paper for gifts.

APRICOT AND APPLE OAT SLICE

Makes approximately 24 pieces

1 cup whole dried apricots
1 cup dried apples
1 cup whole almonds in their skins
1 cup flake coconut
2 cups rolled oats
2 teaspoons orange rind, finely
* grated*
2 teaspoons lemon rind, finely
* grated*
2–4 tablespoons unsweetened
* orange juice*

Chop apricots and dried apple finely in a food processor using the steel blade. While machine is operating, add almonds, coconut, oats, orange and lemon zest. The mixture should resemble coarse breadcrumbs. Slowly add unsweetened orange juice until mixture just starts to stick together.

Press firmly into a 8 inch x 12 inch foil lined pan. Use a glass to roll mixture down firmly in the pan. Refrigerate. Cut into squares or shapes and keep refrigerated.

APPLE AND DATE BARS

Makes approximately 24 bars

Pastry

2 cups wholemeal plain flour
2 cups rolled oats
1/2 cup cold pressed oil
1/4 cup apple juice concentrate
1/2 cup unsweetened orange juice or
 1/2 unsweetened orange juice and
 1/2 lemon juice

Filling

8 ounces dates, finely chopped
2 green apples, peeled, cored and
 sliced
1 cup unsweetened orange juice
1 teaspoon orange rind, finely
 grated

Combine flour and oats in a food processor and process lightly. Add oil and apple juice concentrate and orange juice. Process until pastry binds together. Divide in half. Roll out pastry to make two rectangles. One should be approximately 8 inch x 12 inch, the other slightly bigger. Place the larger piece of pastry on the base of a 8 inch x 12 inch foil lined slice tray.

Place all ingredients in a small pan. Simmer for 20 minutes or until mixture is soft and most of the orange juice absorbed. Cool slightly.

Pour over base and spread evenly. Carefully cover with the top piece of pastry so that it does not break. Press down at the edges to meet the bottom layer. Cook at 350°F for 20–30 minutes. Cool on tray before cutting into bars.

APRICOT CRUMBLE SLICE

Makes 20–24 pieces

Base

1 cup wholemeal plain flour (80%)
1 cup rolled oats
1/4 cup cold pressed oil
2 tablespoons apple juice
 concentrate

Filling

8 ounces dried apricots
1 cup water
1 teaspoon orange rind, finely
 grated

Crumble topping

2 egg whites
4 ounces almonds, finely ground
1 teaspoon vanilla
2 tablespoons apple juice
 concentrate
2 tablespoons flake coconut

To make base   Combine all ingredients in a food processor and process until ingredients bind together. Firmly press into a 8 inch x 12 inch pan. Set aside.

To make filling   Put apricots, water and orange rind in a pan. Simmer until apricots are soft (approximately 10–15 minutes). Purée and cool slightly. Pour over base.

To make topping   Beat egg whites until stiff peaks form. Fold in all other ingredients as they are listed. Pour over apricot filling. Cook at 350°F for 20–25 minutes or until top is firm and lightly brown.

APRICOT NIBBLES

Makes approximately 20

3/4 cup dried apricots
3/4 cup flake coconut
1 teaspoon lemon rind, grated
1 teaspoon orange rind, grated
1 tablespoon unsweetened orange juice
extra shredded coconut, toasted

Cover apricots with boiling water and stand 10 minutes. Drain off liquid. Mince apricots and mix in lightly with the coconut in a food blender. Add remaining ingredients. Knead until well blended. If mixture is too dry add more orange juice. If mixture is too wet add more coconut. Shape into small balls and roll in toasted coconut. Refrigerate.

PRUNE BARS

Makes approximately 24

2/3 cup prunes, finely chopped
1/3 cup dried apple, finely chopped
1 tablespoon sunflower seeds
1 tablespoon sesame seeds, toasted
1/2 cup rolled oats or rolled wheat flakes
1/2 cup raw bran
1 cup almonds in their skins
1/2 cup skim milk powder
1 tablespoon vanilla
1/3 cup unsweetened orange juice
2 teaspoons lemon rind, finely grated

Combine the first 8 ingredients in a food processor and chop roughly. Add vanilla and orange juice to bind. Add lemon rind. Line a 8 inch x 12 inch cookie sheet with foil and press mixture into it. Refrigerate for at least 4 hours. Cut into bars.

GRANOLA FRUIT BARS

Makes 12

2 cups rolled oats
1 cup wholemeal plain flour
1 teaspoon baking powder
1/2–1 teaspoon allspice
1/2 teaspoon cinnamon
2 cups assorted dried fruits (apricots, apples, pears)
1/2 cup sunflower seeds
1/2 cup apple juice concentrate
1/4 cup cold pressed oil
3 egg whites, lightly beaten

Combine the first 7 ingredients and mix well. Stir through the apple juice concentrate and oil. Add egg whites and mix well. Line a 8" x 12" slice tray with non-stick baking paper. Press mixture onto tray and flatten down. Mark into 12 bars with sharp knife. Cook at 400°F for 15–20 minutes. Cool. Cut into bars.

CAROB HEDGEHOG BALLS

1 cup rolled dates
1 cup raisins
1 cup whole almonds in their skins
2 cups rolled oats
1 cup flake coconut
2 tablespoons carob powder
1 tablespoon vanilla
1 tablespoon apple juice concentrate
   or unsweetened orange juice

Place dates and raisins in food processor and cut into small pieces. Add almonds, rolled oats, coconut and carob powder. Process until mixture resembles breadcrumbs. Add vanilla. Mixture should now begin to stick together. Stop motor and check if the texture is correct by taking a small amount in the palm of your hand and rolling it firmly into a ball. If mixture does not bind, add 1 tablespoon apple juice concentrate or unsweetened orange juice. Mixture should not be too sticky. Roll into small balls and refrigerate until firm. Keep in the freezer and use as required.

BANANA LOGS

6 ounces dried banana
3 ounces dried apple
1 cup almonds in their skins
1 cup rolled oats
1/2 cup flake coconut
3 tablespoons apple juice
   concentrate
squeeze of lemon or orange juice
extra flake coconut

Chop banana and apple roughly in a food processor using the steel blade. Add all ingredients except apple juice concentrate. Process until mixture resembles coarse breadcrumbs.

Add apple juice concentrate. Process lightly. If the mixture is too dry add a squeeze of lemon or orange juice. Mixture will come together in your hands. Roll into log shapes approximately 2 inch–3 inch long. Roll in coconut. Store in the freezer.

BASIC OAT MUNCHIES

Makes 20–24

2 cups wholemeal rolled oats
1 cup wholemeal plain flour
1 teaspoon baking powder
1/2 teaspoon allspice
1/2 teaspoon cinnamon
1 cup assorted dried fruits
1/4 cup sunflower seeds
1/2 cup apple juice concentrate
1/4 cup cold pressed almond oil
2 egg whites, lightly beaten

Combine the first 7 ingredients in a large bowl. Combine the last 3 ingredients. Mix until mixture is well combined and sticky. Place spoonful mounds on a non-stick baking sheet. Bake at 400°F for 10–15 minutes until golden.

Opposite:
Granola fruit bars (p131) Apricot crumble slice (p130)
Basic oat munchies (p132) Apple and date bars (p130)
Apricot and apple oat slice (p129) Banana logs (p132)
Carob hedgehog balls (p132)

JAMS, CHUTNEYS AND SAUCES

TOMATO SAUCE

Makes approximately 8½ cups

6½ pound ripe tomatoes, peeled and
    seeds removed
2 large onions, chopped finely
3 large green apples, peeled and
    chopped
2 large carrots, grated
1 cup vinegar
1 cup water
½ teaspoon mace
⅛ teaspoon ground cloves
¼ teaspoon cayenne pepper

Combine all ingredients in a large pan and bring to a boil. Then simmer uncovered for 1 to 1½ hours or until sauce is thick, stirring occasionally. Remove from heat. Purée in a food processor. Pour into bottles. Cool. Keep in refrigerator.

WHITE SAUCE

1 cup skim milk
2 tablespoons cornstarch
black pepper to taste

Some Variations
2 tablespoons grated low fat cheese
2 tablespoons chives, chopped
1 tablespoon parsley, chopped
2 teaspoons dijon mustard
2 teaspoons dill, chopped
2 teaspoons mint, chopped
squeeze of lemon

Pour all but 2 tablespoons milk into pan and bring to the boil. Mix cornstarch with remaining milk until smooth. Just as bubbles appear prior to boiling, add the paste mixture and beat well. Season with black pepper.

Opposite:
Barley water (p140) Carob milkshake (p139)
Peppermint refresher (p140) Banana milkshake (p138)
Pink fizz (p140) Lemonade (p140)

STRAWBERRY JAM

4 green apples
8 ounces strawberries
2 cups unsweetened orange juice
1/2–1 teaspoon cinnamon
rind of 1 orange (optional)

Peel and core apples. Slice finely or grate and place in pan. Wash strawberries and add to apples. Add orange juice, cinnamon and orange rind. Slowly bring to the boil and gently boil for approx 40 minutes or until liquid and fruit become thick. Pour into sterilized jars. Cool and seal. Once the seal is opened the strawberry spread should be kept refrigerated.

SWEET AND SOUR SAUCE

1 can vegetable juice
1/2 cup unsweetened pineapple juice
1/2 cup unsweetened pineapple
2 tablespoons wine vinegar
black pepper
1 teaspoon cornstarch or 2
   tablespoons tomato paste
1/2 cup red and green chopped bell
   pepper

Combine all ingredients, stirring frequently, and bring to a boil. Boil gently until sauce thickens. Garnish with parsley or chives. Use over chicken, fish or vegetables.

TOMATO RELISH

3 1/2 pounds ripe tomatoes
1 pound mild onions
2 cups unsweetened orange juice
3 teaspoons curry powder
1/4 teaspoon chilli powder
1 tablespoon dry mustard
2 cups wine or cider vinegar
1 cup raisins (optional)

Skin tomatoes and remove seeds. Cut into cubes. Peel onions, chop finely. Place tomatoes, onions and orange juice into a large pan. Combine curry powder, chilli powder and mustard with a small amount of orange juice. Add this to the tomato and onions and add vinegar. Slowly bring to a boil over low heat. Boil for 5 minutes. Reduce heat and simmer for an hour or until mixture has thickened. Pour relish into sterilized jars, cool and seal. Store in the refrigerator.

APPLE JAM

8 ounces dried apples
3 cups unsweetened pineapple juice
1/2 lemon
2 teaspoons lemon rind
2 teaspoons cinnamon

Combine all ingredients in a large pan and simmer over gentle heat until apples are soft. Purée the mixture in a blender and pour into sterilized jars. When cool, seal and store in the refrigerator.

APRICOT JAM

8 ounces dried apricots
1 cup water or unsweetened orange juice
2 teaspoons orange rind, finely grated
1 tbsp apple juice concentrate (optional)

Place all ingredients in a small pan and simmer until apricots are soft (approximately 20 minutes). Purée and store in sterilized jars in the refrigerator.

BLUEBERRY SAUCE

12 ounces blueberries
1/4 teaspoon zest of lemon
1 tablespoon arrowroot mixed with a small amount of pear juice to make a paste
2 teaspoons lemon juice
2 cups natural unsweetened pear juice

Cook blueberries in pear juice with lemon juice and lemon rind. As it slowly comes to a boil, add arrowroot and stir until sauce thickens. If a thicker sauce is desired, add more arrowroot.

Use on wholemeal pancakes or over homemade ice cream. It is especially good with baked apples.

DATE AND APPLE CHUTNEY

*4 medium apples peeled, cored and
  grated*
1 pound pitted dates, chopped
2 onions, finely chopped
1 cup raisins or apricots
1 teaspoon chilli powder
2 cups unsweetened orange juice
6 whole cloves
1/4 teaspoon ground allspice
1 1/2 cups wine or cider vinegar

Place all ingredients in a large pan and bring slowly to a boil over low heat. Simmer, stirring occasionally for 1 hour or until a thick, soft consistency. Spoon into sterilized hot jars and seal when cold. Store in the refrigerator. The flavor will improve if left for at least a week before using.

This is an excellent savory spread for sandwiches; use as a dip for vegetable and fruit platters, or as a chutney with chicken, fish or vegetable loaves.

MANGO CHUTNEY

*flesh of 2 mangoes (approximately
  12 ounces)*
2 green apples, peeled and grated
1 onion, peeled and diced
*1 teaspoon fresh ginger, finely
  chopped*
*1/4 cup water or chicken stock (see
  page 31)*
1 cup unsweetened orange juice
*1/3 cup brown rice vinegar
  (macrobiotic, available at health
  food stores)*
1/2 teaspoon chilli powder
1/2 teaspoon cumin
rind of 1 orange
1/2 cup apple juice concentrate

Simmer onion and ginger in chicken stock for 5 minutes. Add all other ingredients. Cover and bring to a boil. Remove lid and cook for 1 hour. Stir frequently to prevent chutney sticking to the base of pan. Cool. Pour into sterilized jars. Keep refrigerated.

DRINKS

Most commercially sold soft drinks are loaded with sugar and artificial flavorings and colorings. You can make your own carbonated drinks at home by mixing 1 part unsweetened natural fruit juice, which is high in vitamin C, with 2 parts mineral water or club soda.

Try orange, pineapple, apple, dark grape, grapefruit, orange and mango, and your own combinations of any of these juices. Serve over ice.

To make clear ice cubes, fill ice trays with hot water. Add pieces of fresh fruit such as strawberries, cherries, pineapple pieces or grapes to the ice block tray and freeze.

JUICES

Freshly squeezed or extracted fruit and vegetable juices make the most delicious and nutritious drinks. Some fruits and vegetables which cannot be squeezed can be placed in a juice extractor which extracts the juice from the pulp with a rotary crushing action.

The pulp remaining is mainly fruit fiber and can be added to the juice for complete food value. Fruit pulp can also be added to cakes for extra moisture or vegetable pulp to soups for added flavor. However, do not store the pulp. It loses its color, taste and nutritional value.

Fruits to juice	Vegetables to juice	Combinations
orange	carrot	orange and pineapple
grapefruit	celery	orange and grapefruit
lemon	tomato	apple and carrot
apple	cucumber	apple and celery
watermelon		tomato and cucumber
pineapple		
grape		All citrus juices combine well.
apricot		

APPLE MILK DRINK

Serves 2

1 cup apple juice, well chilled
1 cup skim milk, well chilled or soy
   milk
sprinkle of cinnamon on top

Blend until thick and foamy.

BANANA MILKSHAKE (1)

Serves 1

1 cup skim milk or soy milk
1 mashed banana
2 teaspoons skim milk powder
1 teaspoon brewer's yeast
sprinkle of nutmeg on top

Place all ingredients in a blender and process until thick and foamy.

BANANA MILKSHAKE (2)

Serves 1

1 small ripe banana (can be frozen)
1 cup skim milk or soy milk
1/2 teaspoon vanilla
dash of nutmeg (optional)
4 ice cubes

Chop banana roughly. Place all ingredients into a food blender or processor. Blend until smooth and frothy. The milkshake will be frothier and creamy smooth if you use frozen bananas.

Make this milkshake into a banana smoothie by substituting 1 cup of non-fat yogurt for the skim milk.

STRAWBERRY MILKSHAKE

Serves 2

1 cup strawberries
2 tablespoons unsweetened orange
   juice
1 tablespoon apple juice concentrate
2 cups ice cold skim milk
1/2 cup non-fat yogurt or 2
   tablespoon skim milk powder

Simmer strawberries in orange juice and apple juice until strawberries are soft. Cool. Purée all ingredients and serve.

APRICOT MILKSHAKE

Makes approximately 2 servings

1 cup ice cold skim milk, soy milk or
    goat's milk
1/2 cup fresh apricots, finely chopped
    or natural sugar free canned
    apricots
2 ice cubes
1 teaspoon apple juice concentrate
1/4 teaspoon cinnamon (optional)

Place all ingredients in a food blender or processor and blend until thick and creamy. Add 2 tablespoons low fat ricotta cheese for a richer, creamier thick-shake.

BERRY COMBINATION MILKSHAKE

1 cup well-chilled non-fat milk
1/4 cup well chilled non-fat yogurt
1 cup mixed berries (blueberries,
    strawberries, raspberries,
    loganberries, blackberries)
1 teaspoon apple juice concentrate

Combine all ingredients in a food blender or processor and blend until thick and frothy.

CAROB MILKSHAKE

Serves 2

1 cup well chilled skim milk
2 tablespoons skim milk powder
1 tablespoon carob powder
1 teaspoon vanilla
nutmeg
1/2 banana, chopped (optional)

Place all ingredients in a food blender or processor and blend until smooth and frothy. Pour into a tall glass full of ice cubes. Garnish with a sprinkle of nutmeg.

APRICOT AND VANILLA DRINK

Serves 1

1 cup skim milk or soy milk
4 fresh apricots, pitted
1 teaspoon vanilla

Blend thoroughly until thick and foamy.

LEMONADE

Serves 6

1/2 cup lemon juice (2 1/2 lemons)
1/4 cup apple juice concentrate
club soda or mineral water
ice cubes

Mix the lemon and apple juice together. Fill glass with ice cubes. Add 2 tablespoons lemon mixture. Pour in mineral water or club soda. To increase quantities slightly reduce apple juice concentrate. That is, 2 cups lemon juice to 3/4 cup apple juice concentrate.

BARLEY WATER

3 tablespoons pearl barley
enough water to cover
9 additional cups water
juice and peel of 2 oranges
juice and peel of 2 lemons
1 tablespoon honey

Cover barley with water. Bring to a boil, strain and discard water. Cover barley with 9 cups of water, bring to a boil and simmer for 15 minutes.

In a large jug, add honey, juice and peel of oranges and lemons. Pour barley water in through a sieve. Discard barley. Leave to cool. Remove peel and refrigerate.

This is an excellent thirst quencher or a pick-me-up if you're not feeling well.

PEPPERMINT REFRESHER

Serves 1

1/2 cup cold peppermint tea
1/2 cup ice cold club soda
ice cubes
peppermint or fresh mint leaves to
  garnish

Add soda to peppermint tea and garnish with ice cubes and leaves.

PINK FIZZ

Serves 1

1/2 cup watermelon
1 cup ice cold club soda

Remove seeds of watermelon and push the flesh through a fine sieve. Add club soda to watermelon and serve with pink straws and a pink parasol.

BREAKFAST

ORANGE GRAPEFRUIT

Serves 1

1/2 grapefruit
1 slice orange

Put the slice of orange on top of the grapefruit. Cover with plastic wrap and refrigerate overnight. This procedure allows the natural sweetness of the grapefruit and orange to combine and give a very sweet fruit.

To serve cut a slit in the slice of orange from its center to the outside and twist to stand orange up on grapefruit.

Serve with a cup of hot lemon water (cup of hot water and a slice of lemon).

CITRUS SEGMENTS

Serves 1

1/2 orange
1/2 grapefruit
juice of 1 orange
2 teaspoons finely grated lemon rind
mint leaves to garnish

Using a sharp knife, pare the peel and pith from orange and grapefruit. To cut segments, cut on either side of the membrane and remove segments. Arrange segments on a plate. Place juice and rind in a small pan and heat, but do not boil. Stir lemon rind into juice while heating. Remove from heat. Let cool, but not necessarily to get cold. Pour juice over fruit segments, garnish with mint leaves and serve.

YOGURT POTS

Serves 1

1 cup natural non-fat yogurt
1/4 cup cooked fruit (apples, pears, plums, rhubarb, apricots)
2 tablespoons suitable spread
1/2 teaspoon vanilla

Choose a container (preferably ceramic as it retains a perfect chilled temperature) that is at least 1 cup capacity and has a lid.

Place cooked fruit on the base of the pot. Combine yogurt, spread of your choice and vanilla. Lightly stir. Pour over fruit. Place lid on top. Keep in refrigerator for at least 24 hours to let flavors blend. Remove lid and serve in the pot.

OATMEAL

Serves 1

1/2 cup rolled oats
1 cup water
1 teaspoon vanilla

Combine all ingredients in a small pan. Slowly bring to a boil. Simmer for 3 minutes, stirring continuously. Pour into a bowl. Serve with fruits, or a small amount of fruit juice.

MUSHROOM AND TOMATO ROLLS

Serves 4

4 wholemeal bread rolls, remove tops
*   and hollow out the centers*
10 ounces mushrooms, peeled
1/2 cup water
4 cooked tomatoes and juice
*   (approximately 1/4 cup)*
2 tablepoons chopped parsley
2 tablespoons chopped chives or 1/4
*   cup chopped green onions*
pinch of nutmeg (optional)
1/4 cup water
2 tablespoons cornstarch

Cook mushrooms in 1/2 cup water over a gentle heat for 1/4 hour. Add tomatoes and juice, parsley and chives. Cook for a further 5 minutes. Add nutmeg. Mix cornstarch and stir into mushrooms to thicken.

Place rolls under broiler until well browned top and bottom. Place each roll on individual serving plates and spoon mushroom and tomato mixture into each roll.

HOMEMADE TOASTED GRANOLA AND FRESH FRUIT

Makes approximately 6 cups

Allow 1/2 cup homemade toasted granola and a piece of fresh fruit per person

1 cup wheat flakes
2 cups rolled oats
1 1/2 cups unprocessed bran
1/2 cup raw coconut
1/2 cup wheat germ (optional)
1/4 cup skim milk powder
2 ounces currants
2 ounces raisins
2 ounces finely cut dried apricots
2 ounces finely cut dried peaches

Place the first five ingredients on a large baking tray. Spread out evenly. Place in a very hot oven for 5–10 minutes or until browning begins. Turn over once and leave for a further 3–5 minutes. Do not burn. Remove from oven and spread out on paper to cool.

When completely cool, place in a container with remaining ingredients and mix well. Make sure the container is well sealed.

Fresh Fruit   Sliced banana, peach or pear would be an excellent choice in fresh fruit.

FRUIT PLATTER

Serves 1

Some Selections

2 pineapple circles
8 strawberries
4 kiwi fruit quarters
1 whole pear

1 peach
8 strawberries
1 nectarine
1 banana

1 fig
1 banana
1 small bunch of green grapes
1 apple

12 cherries
2 apricots
1 plum
1 apple

1 fig
kiwi fruit slices
bunch of purple grapes
tangerine segments

slices of papaya
berries of choice
slices of honeydew melon
cantaloupe balls

There is no better way to start the day than with the flavors of fresh fruits. Choose 4 different varieties of fruit, depending on what is in season. Take a little time to arrange them attractively on the platter and always serve the fruit chilled.

CINNAMON PEARS

Serves 4

4 pears
1¹/₂ cups apple juice, unsweetened
rind of 1 lemon
¹/₂ teaspoon cinnamon

Peel whole pears and leave stems on. Stand pears up in a pan. Pour over apple juice, lemon rind and cinnamon. Place lid on pan and simmer over very gentle heat until just tender. Serve warm.

INDEX